GUYS

TOUGH GUYS

JOHN WYATT

Schiffer Publishing Ltd

4880 Lower Valley Road • Atglen, PA 19310

Another Schiffer Books by the Author:
Under My Skin.
ISBN: 0-7643-1713-X. $39.95

Another Schiffer Books on Related Subjects:
Hard Boys and Bad Girls,
Lives of Aspiring Wrestlers.
Thomas McGovern.
ISBN: 978-0-7643-3437-5. $24.99

Designed by Justin Watkinson
Type set in Zurich BT/Zurich BT

ISBN: 978-0-7643-4522-7
Printed in China

Published by Schiffer Publishing, Ltd.
4880 Lower Valley Road
Atglen, PA 19310
Phone: (610) 593-1777; Fax: (610) 593-2002
E-mail: Info@schifferbooks.com

For our complete selection of fine books on this and related subjects, please visit our website at www.schifferbooks.com. You may also write for a free catalog.

This book may be purchased from the publisher. Please try your bookstore first.

We are always looking for people to write books on new and related subjects. If you have an idea for a book, please contact us at
proposals@schifferbooks.com

Schiffer Publishing's titles are available at special discounts for bulk purchases for sales promotions or premiums. Special editions, including personalized covers, corporate imprints, and excerpts can be created in large quantities for special needs. For more information, contact the publisher.

CONTENTS

FOREWORD
THE TOUGH GUY

"Tough guy." Just saying those two words alone conjures up images shaped by preconceived notion and connotation and—of course—the idea that throughout runs the common denominator of "badassery." The tough guy is an ideal come to life, a label, a badge of honor, or distinction. A description that encapsulates fistfights and intimidation and the kind of threats that are wordless and unspoken. The tough guy promises violence—whether it be somewhere in his sordid past, his daunting present, or his menacing future.

The tough guy can manifest in any number of ways and in any number of people. It can take the form of the seasoned boxer, or the underground mixed martial artist, or the street fighter, or the bounty hunter, or the biker. And, it can cross gender lines, with the label transforming into one fittingly affixed to a gal of similar renown.

"Tough guy" is as amorphous a term as it is descriptive, though. For what traits specifically go into constructing the tough guy? Must the subject sport ink on their forearms and callouses on their knuckles? Must he know a dozen katas or what the canvas in an aged boxing gym smells like? Should he be well-acquainted with the inside of a jail cell or the vista within a cage of the ultimate fighting variety? It is impossible to ascribe to the tough guy any particular necessary qualities. To paraphrase US Supreme Court Justice Potter Stewart in his infamous quote on the definition of "obscenity," you can't succeed in intelligibly defining it, but when it comes to the tough guy, you damn well know one when you see one.

John Wyatt knows one when he sees one, too.

In his first book, *Under My Skin*, the veteran lensman photographed individuals who were heavily tattooed—an endeavor that at times skirted the realm of the tough guy. But the seeds of inspiration for this book were planted long before that project, and in a soil enriched by the fights (both in and out of the ring) of boxing legend Chuck Wepner—as well as a desire to capture those "great photographs never taken." Those seeds grew into the photos contained in the book you hold in your hands today.

For *Tough Guys*, John sought out his subjects in their natural habitat, where they were most at ease and most willing to talk—hence the interviews that accompany many of the photos. There's Gerry Cooney, the former top pro heavyweight boxer; there's Rob Kaman, the famed Dutch kickboxer; there's Vince Marchetti, the martial artist; and there's Peter Storm, the underground fighter and promoter. There are, of course, others, which is a testament to the breadth and width of John's pursuit. It's all there, in a visual feast of still frames and implied violence.

Read the words and soak in the images. *Tough Guys* captures it all, and does so perfectly.

—Jim Genia
author of *Raw Combat: The Underground World of Mixed Martial Arts*

ACKNOWLEDGMENTS

I would like to thank everyone who appears in this book for their time and patience. I've learned something from everyone and have always walked away from each meeting knowing that my life was enriched by the experience. A few were friends, some have become friends, but all made me feel like I was visiting an old friend. They gave me energy and more motivation for this project. From the fight world, I particularly want to thank Chuck Wepner for his support and assistance. I am very grateful to Ricardo Liborio, one of the nicest and most memorable people I have ever met. He gave me access to his gym, American Top Team, and his fighters. His insight as a former champion and coach was invaluable. I also owe thanks to Vincent Marchetti and Rob Guarino for their support and help.

I am thankful to Donald Lokuta for referring me to Barbara Burn, who was the perfect person to edit my interviews. I am grateful to her for her insight into my project and her fine editing skills. I am also grateful to several others who helped bring this project to fruition. Valeri Larko helped make sense out of the order of the photographs and was able to edit them until I had the best fit for the book. Bob Bernstein generously gave his support and hours of help in editing both the text and the photographs. Owen Kanzler provided supportive enthusiasm for my project and helpful insights regarding my photographs and text. Shelby Lee Adams and Nick Bubash offered their encouragement and helpful suggestions. My son, Mike, and my daughter, Kate Wyatt Hammond, showed constant interest in this project and proffered writing suggestions, input, and support. Joseph Schembri and Howard Zoubek contributed technical support. Steve Proctor, Hugo Estenssoro, Vicki Orlando, Ruth Kantor, Grace Brophy, and Don Mokrauer were sources of writing ideas and help, and numerous other friends and acquaintances offered much encouragement and many helpful suggestions.

I would like to thank Pete Schiffer for his enthusiasm for my book and his willingness to publish it. Also, Jeff Snyder, my editor at Schiffer Publishing, for his kindness and guidance in the editing process.

In memory of Richie Trainor, a tough guy to the end.
For my son, Mike Wyatt, and my daughter, Kate Wyatt Hammond.

INTRODUCTION

I have been a boxing fan since childhood. My fascination with fighting began on Friday nights in Brooklyn in the 1950s watching bouts on our family's round, black-and-white small-screen television. It was very exciting to watch the fast pace of two skilled boxers as I tried to figure what the outcome would be. It was clear to me even then that anything could happen in a bout. At the same time, I was aware of how different these fighters and their sport were from other athletes and other sports, as they threw and absorbed countless hard punches.

In the late sixties I became further enthralled when I was introduced by my friend Richie Trainor to the reigning New Jersey Heavyweight Boxing Champion, Chuck Wepner. I attended his fights in New York and New Jersey with Richie and his brother, Bob, and we would visit with Chuck in the locker room before the fights. No one epitomized toughness more than Chuck, who in his career endured hundreds of stitches and seventeen broken noses. As the consummate competitor, however, he would continue to press an opponent no matter what physical obstacles he encountered.

I witnessed Chuck's fight with Sonny Liston at the Jersey City Armory, when Chuck had so much blood in his eyes that all he could see was a dark shadow, yet he kept coming at Liston. The referee, fearing for Chuck's well being, stopped the action to see if he could continue. Thanks to a feat of in-ring creativity, Chuck's manager, Al Braverman, poked Chuck three times in the back when the referee asked Chuck how many fingers he was holding up. The fight was later stopped before the tenth round, however, when the doctor realized that Chuck would need at least seventy stitches. Chuck was angry that the fight was stopped. He wanted to continue. Later in his career, Chuck fought Muhammad Ali, and was one of the few boxers who went fifteen rounds with him. There aren't many boxers who can say they did that. Sylvester Stallone would later base his movie *Rocky* on Chuck and his courageous tenacity in that fight.

During those times, I witnessed many Damon Runyonesque scenes, such as the time I saw Willie Gilzenberg, an old fight promoter, in the back of a bar in Jersey City with stacks of money on a dimly lit pool table doling out shares to the fighters. Although I had not yet discovered my passion for photography, my memories are just as vivid as photographs. As time went on, my interest evolved, and I found myself watching mixed martial arts on video, even before it became a mainstream televised event.

Fighters are a very rare commodity. During a battle, the potential always exists for severe injury or even death. Most fighters tell me they have fought at one time or another with injuries that they received in training before a fight. Their biggest fear is a bad public performance, like being outclassed by a superior opponent. There is no place to hide one's mistakes.

When I began exhibiting the photographs, I would get comments like, "Aren't you afraid to be alone with these people?" or "Didn't they all have bad childhoods?" These stereotypical views are far off the mark. The backgrounds of these fighters mirror the rest of society. Some come from poverty, some from the middle class, and some from the upper middle class. Many have college degrees and some have left professional careers to pursue fighting full time. Some grew up in poor neighborhoods and were forced to fight or become victims. When they realized they were good at fighting, they began training for competition.

Throughout the project, I became increasingly impressed with many of the finer attributes of these fighters. They were kind, sincere, and professional. They were all open, genuine, humble, and personable.

This book is a mix of professional competitors and colorful characters, including bouncers and barroom brawlers. Some are well known, but others are less familiar or completely unknown, because I didn't set out to compile a book of celebrity competitors. My overriding criterion was their toughness. I wanted to showcase fighters who did their best and never quit. Many of the fighters in this book are active in the ring and cage today, and some work as expert trainers and skill teachers.

And all of them are tough!

Chuck Wepner, Bayonne, New Jersey

CHUCK WEPNER is a former heavyweight professional boxer who was a top ten contender. He fought Muhammad Ali for fifteen rounds in a title fight and was the inspiration for the movie *Rocky.*

When my mother and father split, my mother, my younger brother, and I moved from New York to Bayonne, New Jersey, to live with my grandparents. They had no room for us in their apartment, so they converted a coal shed in the basement into a little one-room apartment. We used to bathe in a big cement sink where my grandfather washed the mops. He was the superintendent of the building. It was very crowded in the main apartment—thirteen people lived there, including my grandparents, so we were only allowed in on Sundays, when we all ate together. We lived there until I was twelve, when we moved to the projects.

When I was sixteen, a kid named Mousy came down to the basketball court behind the projects—I played a lot of basketball in those days. He grabbed my basketball and stuck a switchblade in it, so I beat him up. Mousy ran in Freddie Linquist's gang. Two hours later, I'm in my apartment on the fourth floor, and I hear some guy calling to me, "Come on down. You beat up Mousy and I'm going to break your fucking head." It was Freddie Linquist with his gang. Freddie was the toughest kid in the neighborhood. I remember he had long curly hair. I grabbed him by the hair and punched him in the face three or four times. "You give, you give," I kept yelling, and finally he says, "Yeah, I give." We got up and, believe it or not, we shook hands. After that, I was the toughest kid in the neighborhood. Nobody bothered me again.

I wasn't a bully. I didn't go around looking for people to beat up, but when Mousy punctured my basketball I beat him up, and when Freddie challenged me, I couldn't very well run away, could I? A year later, I was seventeen and I joined the Marine Corps, where I got some training fighting in smokers. Then came the Golden Gloves, the New Jersey Championship, and the North American Championship, all of which I won. I've held four different titles, you know. I've been lucky.

I was a street fighter, too. A lot of times I got into fights with guys bigger than me. You don't see too many guys that are smaller who pick on someone six foot five and a half, 240 pounds. A lot of guys out there are troublemakers; they'll look for trouble or to make a reputation. When you're a former heavyweight champion and you've fought for the title, they think "I'd like to beat this guy. I'd like to beat up Chuck Wepner." I've always had the reputation of being a very tough street fighter. I never lost in the street, and that's one of my standard jokes: "I'm undefeated in alleys, telephone booths, and men's rooms."

I was in the top ten of the world for forty-two straight months, and when I fought Muhammad Ali, I was ranked seventh in the world. Yeah, I was a contender. You had to be a contender to get a shot for the title. I wasn't supposed to fight Ali; it was supposed to be George Foreman. I had beaten Ernie Terrell for the North American Heavyweight Championship, and Don King said, "I'm going to send you out to Salt Lake City. If you beat Hinkie [Terrible Terry Hinkie], I'll set you up for a fight with Foreman for the title." And I beat Hinkie. Bob Hope was the host of the show (one dollar from every ticket went to the Biafra Fund). It was a brawl, the whole fight. I had him down seven times. It was a twelve-rounder, and I knocked him out in the eleventh round.

Afterward, in the dressing room, Bob Hope walked in. I was lying on the table and Bob Hope touched my hand. "Chuck," he said, "I just wanted to let you know that's the greatest heavyweight fight I've ever seen." After the fight, Don King says, "Okay, you earned it. Great fight, Chuck. You're going to be fighting George Foreman for the title. So stay in shape. Don't party too much." Only it wasn't Foreman I fought, but Ali.

A few weeks later, Ali comes out of retirement, goes to Zaire, and stuns the world, knocking out Foreman in the eighth round when everyone thought Foreman would win. Don King calls me two days later and says, "My brother, my man"—that's the way he talked—"I love you, my brother. I promised you a shot at the title, and you're going to get it." Anyway, three months and a day later, I'm sitting at home watching *Kojak* and the phone rings. It's my mother. "Mom, I told you never to call me during *Kojak*." I loved Telly Savalas. And she says, "Did you see the *Daily News*? The back page. Ali to defend against Wepner." I hung up the phone, threw on my clothes, jumped in my car, and drove to the Embassy Theater in Bayonne, where they sold papers out front. I picked up a paper and showed it to the news vendor. He says, "Holy Christ, Chuck, that's great," and he gives me the paper for free. I think they were twenty five cents back then.

Every day there was TV, radio, magazines, newspapers. I had five or six different newspapers and TV people at the training camp. And my picture was on the cover of *Sports Illustrated*. Neil Leifer was the photographer and he said to me, "I want to take some pictures of you. I'm going to spray you, so it looks like sweat dripping down." And he put the lights underneath to make me look evil. It won "Picture of the Year" and "Picture of the Decade" for Neil Leifer. Then he was made the chief photographer for *Life*.

The biggest thing for me in my career, I think, was my condition. I trained very hard. I knew that I never had a lot of talent, like an Ali or a Kenny Norton, or a George Foreman. I didn't have the skills because I never had real training; I never had a manager, so I had to depend on condition and what I call balls. First of all, you can't go into a fight being afraid. I was never afraid in a fight, not even with Ali. I was afraid of looking bad, you know, making myself look foolish because I was outclassed. I don't think that ever really happened to me in a fight. The closest was maybe Muhammad Ali where he looked a lot better than me. But I made up for it because I pressed the fight. They said during the fight, "Ali is super talented. Wepner is super heart and courage." That's the way I fought all my fights.

After the fight, Brent Musburger said that I gained more in my loss to Ali than Ali did in his win. We went fifteen rounds and I had Ali down. Angelo Dundee said on national television that I knocked Ali down, that Ali pulled away from a jab and was off balance. The punch definitely landed. He said, "No matter what they say, the referee called it a legal knockdown. It was a legal knockdown." Angelo was very honest about it.

I trained full time for that fight, and that's the only time. Don King sent me to camp, and I got myself into tremendous shape because I intended to press Ali from the opening bell, and I did. That's the only way I thought I could beat him, wear him down and get him tired, and maybe in the later rounds land a couple good shots and maybe take him out. But to hit Ali with two punches in a row was tough, very tough.

I was never known as a defensive fighter. I could take a punch, but sometimes you're so intent on offense that your defense suffers. My style was aggressive. My manager used to say, "You're too aggressive. Why don't you take one step back to take two steps forward?" I said, "Yeah, but if I don't take the one step back, then I can take three steps forward."

Liston and Foreman and a guy named Horst Geisler, not Ali, were the heaviest hitters I fought. I fought Gisler in Syracuse. The guy was six foot eight, 280 pounds. It was near the end of my career, after the Ali fight. Al Braverman, my cut man, said to me, "He's a big, slow guy. You stick with him and you'll wear him out. But the guy was undefeated—he was 14–0 and a big, big hitter. He saw the opportunity to fight a guy who went fifteen with Ali, and he was in great shape. They stopped that fight on cuts in the eighth round of a ten-rounder.

After the fight, I went out with the guys drinking, and I had a terrific headache for a couple of days. When I got back to Bayonne, I went to the hospital. I had been walking around with a concussion for two days, drinking and partying. One eye was closed, my nose was packed.

It's unfortunate, but I never had a full-time trainer. I used to run in the morning, work all day, and then do more roadwork and gym at night. In my nineteen, twenty years, I must have had six or seven different trainers. And they were just part-time guys who worked in a gym. In *Rocky*, which Stallone wrote after seeing me fight Ali, Burgess Meredith was in charge of the gym, and he trained Rocky on the side until Rocky got to the title bout. Rocky was me—I never had a real trainer.

But I could take a punch. I have a twenty-one inch neck, which acts as a shock absorber. My bone structure is probably a little better than most. My jaw was never broken. I got my eyes cut and my nose broken, but never my jaw. And the pain, the pain thing, I could take. When I got hurt in the ring, it just made me mad, and I'd try a little harder. Some guys get hurt and they back off. Not me.

The only time Al stopped a fight was in Syracuse with Duane Bobick, the Olympic fighter. The commissioner, James Farley, came into the dressing room before the bout. He said, "Wepner, we know you're a dirty roughhouse fighter. No hitting out of the clinch, no rabbit punching." No this, no that. "All right," I said. "I won't do it if he don't do it." He was protecting Bobick, who was undefeated, 21–0.

In the third round, we came out of a clinch. I usually came out throwing punches but I stepped back, and he suckered me with a big left hook and broke my nose. He actually pushed part of the bones from my nose inside my face. I was spitting out chunks of blood. Clots were sticking in my throat, and I was gasping for air. I was choking in the fourth and fifth rounds. I couldn't breathe. Al said to me, "Chuck, I got to stop this. You're going to choke to death in the middle of the round if one of these clots gets stuck in your throat." "No, give me one more round," I said, but he went to the referee and he stopped the bout. So one of the few times in my career I was a gentleman and stepped back without throwing punches coming out of a clinch, I got caught. Bobick was a big left-hooker. Eh, what are you going to do?

Bob Trainor and Chuck Wepner at Kuhl's Tavern, Bayonne, New Jersey.

BOB TRAINOR was a barroom brawler in northern New Jersey, and was often joined by his brother Richie and Chuck Wepner. Bob is 6′ 2″ and 320 pounds and, according to Chuck, was as fast as any middleweight boxer.

MONTE BARRETT is a professional heavyweight boxer. He is the former WBC Continental Americas Heavyweight champion and former WBO Asia Pacific Heavyweight and WBO Oriental Heavyweight champion.

I'm fortunate to have the longevity that I've had in boxing. When I was coming up as an amateur, I met Mike Tyson and Evander Holyfield, and both of them told me that because I started boxing at twenty-two, I wasn't burned out. Some guys have been boxing since they were six or seven years old, and by the time they are eighteen they are professionals and have had three hundred amateur fights. I have had only forty amateur fights, and I'm still learning on the job. The good thing about my whole career is that I have had a lot of time off. I took off five years out of my fourteen years as a professional. My body and my mind have had a chance to rest.

This is not a young man's sport. I know that twenty-eight to thirty-two is the age when your body usually peaks; that's why I have to work extra hard. There is so much science and technology and information out there that your body can go beyond where you thought it could go. I apply myself. If I'm going to do boxing, I'm going to do it to the fullest, because God gave me a gift and I want to nurture it. I want to be the best that I can be, and now more than ever I really have to apply myself. With age comes wisdom, and I think that I'm much smarter than I was in my twenties. I think I'm growing every day. As they say, you always have one more fight in you. I don't want to get to the point that I'm punch drunk. I don't want to get to the point where I don't have all of my faculties, where I can't hold a conversation or enjoy my family

I really don't live in fear. I'm an overachiever and I realize that you can't win everything. You can be good at some things, but you can't be good at everything. So sometimes you are going to have one of those days. In boxing you have only one night, one chance to get it right. It is not a do over, it's not a playoff. Every fight, whether you fight for one dollar or a million, is a championship fight. I'm in a position where I have to be good all the time. When I look back at my fights with Dominick Guinn, Tye Fields, and Phil Jackson, I know I really applied myself. I went to an uncomfortable space with my training, both mentally and spiritually, to get where I wanted to be. Sometimes you have to take yourself out of your comfort zone to be at your best.

As for the pain, I tell people that you've got to get hit in the face a couple of times. Most of the time, when I'm off for a long time and I get hit, I swell up real bad. Nobody wants to get used to getting punched in the face, but that's life. When you're doing something as physical as boxing, you have to get hit to get used to it. So I think we have a higher threshold for pain.

Don King was the most vicious promoter I've ever dealt with, but I have to respect him as a businessman because a lot of promoters act like they love you, like they're your best friend. At least you know where Don's coming from. He gave me the best lesson in boxing, which is that you never get what you're worth, only what you negotiate. And it stuck with me. We were at his table in Boca Raton. He was puffing on a cigar. When he said that, it really stuck with me through my whole career. We feel like we're worth a million bucks, but we're really worth what we negotiate.

KEVIN MULHALL is a 6th degree black belt in Kar-Do jiu jitsu, a 4th degree black belt in Hoteikan jiu jitsu, a 1st degree black belt in Tae Kwon Do. He was a Muay Thai fighter and holds many championships in the martial arts. At the present time, he is a Muay Thai and physical fitness instructor and can be seen in the UFC and other leagues as a referee. Kevin is the owner of Jersey Fight Club, where he teaches Muay Thai.

Being a referee has been a great experience for me, and I really love it. It has kept me involved in the fighting aspect of the sport after I couldn't fight anymore. What makes it so great is that I get to do it with one of my best friends, Big Dan Miriglioto. Dan and I have been reffing together for fifteen years now, and we gradually moved up to bigger and bigger shows. Eventually we did some of the biggest shows in the world: the UFC, the WEC, the IFL, Ring of Combat, King of the Cage. When you've done those shows and traveled around the world and been paid to do the job, it's as if you're being sent on mini-vacations with your best friend to do what you love to do. I couldn't ask for anything more than what I've done. The first time you go to a big show, you're nervous, but when you have your buddy there saying, "Go get it, do a good job," that's a great feeling. I feel more fortunate than some of the other refs to be able to do it this way.

The one thing I strive to do is to reach the top of whatever it is I'm doing. The UFC is known as the biggest, best show in the world, and doing a UFC world championship fight was a great experience for me. That is where I wanted to go, the highest level, a main event for a title in the UFC, the George St. Pierre / Dan Hardy fight. The funny thing is that right after I refereed that fight, I went shopping with my fiancée, and a guy saw that I had a martial arts shirt on and asked me if I liked the fights. I said, "Yeah, I like them." He asked, "Did you watch the fights this weekend?" I said, "Yeah, I watched them. Did you?" He said he watched them, so I asked what his favorite fight was. He said it was the George St. Pierre and Dan Hardy match. He had no idea who I was. I don't have much personality or charisma as a ref, and my fiancée thinks I need more of an image, but I don't mind blending in.

One night when I was watching some fights in a bar, a guy was talking about fighting during one of the events. You could tell that he didn't really know what he was talking about. He started telling me all about some fight, and the funny thing was that I had refereed that fight. He told me what had happened in the fight and what was wrong and what was right. He might even have critiqued me. My friends wanted to tell him who I was, but I stopped them and said, "No, let him keep going." I wanted to hear what he had to say. The guys that tell you the most don't usually know what they are talking about.

The uneducated fan is the worst fan. The educated fans appreciate what's going on because they understand what's happening. The fan who doesn't understand says, "This is boring," because he doesn't get it. The smallest movement can either make or break a move, and you can't always see the subtleties from outside the ring. You can't see a fighter's eyes; you can't see what is happening. There are certain views that only a referee or the other fighter are going to get. You can't capture that on camera. Whenever people ask me what I thought of a particular call, I don't go against the other referee because I couldn't see what he saw. The number one thing is the fighter's eyes. Just because a fighter is still doing moves does not mean that he is conscious. Your motor skills take over when you have been knocked out a lot of times. That's what the non-fighters don't understand. They say "Well, he's still fighting," but they have no clue.

RIGEL BALSAMICO

RIGEL BALSAMICO began boxing training in his native Ireland at the age of five, later trained in Muay Thai in Philadelphia, and was certified as a Kru in Bangkok in 1999. At the age of thirty-six, with a broken foot, he won a decision in Bangkok in front of 150,000 fans gathered for the Queen's Birthday Celebration. While he was still fighting, he formed his own team as a Kru at the Cool Hearts Muay Thai Camp in Philadelphia.

I love rough neighborhoods where fighting is the most popular sport. In the neighborhoods where I have lived, even after I moved to America, fistfights were just part of what we did. We fought and the next day maybe we were friends. It was like a no-hard-feelings kind of thing. There's definitely something to basement boxing. Our heroes were fighters; our heroes were boxers. My brother, who is fourteen years older than me, is a boxer, and I grew up respecting and fearing him.

I had a violent upbringing. I think that once you've been abused, it has power over you. Somebody can do what they want with you. Well, you don't want anybody in the world to be able to use power over you. You don't want to be beaten; you don't want to be held down. You don't want somebody to be stronger than you, and you definitely don't want to be knocked out.

Boxing in Ireland was much more popular than it is here, since parents were not so afraid for their kids. It was like Little League, and there were athletic clubs everywhere that taught boxing. With kids here getting concussions and rotator cuff and ACL injuries in football and basketball, it seems that amateur boxing is relatively safe, probably safer.

In Ireland I went to monastery schools, and in America, I went to a Catholic school on Long Island. My first day in the neighborhood, we were playing schoolyard sports. One kid, whose name I don't want to say since he's still a friend of mine, a city cop somewhere, and a Special Forces Ranger in the Army, didn't like the way I played. So he came up to me and punched me straight in the jaw. That's how we got to know each other. That was just the way we dealt with things.

I don't say that I learned to fight out of fear, but I am definitely a "neurotic frightened kid" who fought to keep my back against the wall, kind of like a caged animal. I always felt like the underdog. Even when I started ring fighting, won titles, and became pretty well established, I always thought the other guy was doing more or was going to train harder. I always had a certain sense of anxiety, not fear, about the other guy, the opponent. I wanted to knock everybody out.

In 1992, when I was twenty-one years old, I was working in Philadelphia. I had heard of Muay Thai, but at that point it was not well known, and the gym where I taught weight-lifting and fitness had a Muay Thai camp. I didn't have much respect for martial arts back then because I was a street fighter. But Muay Thai was different, much more like boxing. In training, they skip rope, hit bags, and hit pads, but they use everything—knees, elbows. I was blown away. I couldn't believe it.

To be at a highly competitive level in Muay Thai, in Europe or in Thailand, you've got to be in great shape. No dis to boxing, but thuggishness and athleticism can get you by when it's just hands. But when you have elbows, kicks, knees, clinching, and wrestling, it takes a lot more. There's no safe area. You can't just be an outside fighter. It's difficult. We always say the strongest weapon in Muay Thai is your head, and your heart, of course. You can't teach heart. You knock somebody down and they get back up. They have heart. With some people, their nose bleeds in their first fight and they don't want to fight anymore. You can train them, you can teach them technique, but heart . . . that's what gets you through.

CANDICE GONGORA is a Muay Thai fighter. She trains in Philadelphia and trained and fought in Thailand.

I'm a short fighter and I've got a lot going against me. I'm not an athlete. When I started, I weighed 150 pounds. I had a desk job, and I had to do something because I was eighteen years old and I didn't need to be overweight. I don't really catch on that fast, but I'm tough, and I guess that's what matters the most. Every time I step in, I just get hit, but you just gotta keep going, keep moving forward

Before I started Muay Thai, I took karate for a little while and I didn't like it very much. I wanted something that would challenge me more and, like, break me down, physically, emotionally, that would really just pick me apart so that I could see where my strengths are and who I really am. Rigel was teaching at a place right in my hometown in New Jersey, and I just stumbled in one day. I saw that they had Muay Thai and other types of martial arts. We talked for a very long time, and he got me to come in and take his class. And from then on, I never stopped. I took the class every single day, and from the start I was training six days a week.

I'm not worried about my face, honestly; I'm not really that vain about it. I've never gotten cut, though I've had plenty of black eyes. I've been elbowed in the face but I didn't cut. And I don't bruise very easily on my face, so I don't worry too much about that.

I went to Thailand for a month two years ago, and that's where I dislocated my shoulder the first time sparring with a really tall Dutch girl. I threw a jab and she nearly knocked my arm off. But I fought with my arm like that and it didn't come out, so it was cool.

Training over there was awesome. We were in Chiang Mai, all the way up north in the mountains. It was really beautiful. The camps are open, and it's all outside. There are stray dogs everywhere and vendors with fresh pineapple, and it's just amazing.

I had a match with a Thai who was fourteen years old and had forty fights. She kicked my ass, but it was good. I kept going; I didn't stop or anything. They stopped the fight in the third round because she kept kicking me in my head. But the girl she fought before me, the Dutch girl who had dislocated my arm, quit because the Thai girl kept her on her stomach and she started crying. I felt better that it didn't happen to me.

My chest tattoo reads: "My head is bloody but unbowed." I was at the fights one night in New York, and the poem "Invictus" by William Henley was printed across the wall where we were all warming up. I wasn't fighting that night, but my friends were warming up and waiting to fight.

> In the fell clutch of circumstance
> I have not winced nor cried aloud.
> Under the bludgeonings of chance
> My head is bloody, but unbowed.

That poem just gives me chills. I love it. It's for somebody who fights, or even is just in training. If you don't put your blood, sweat, and tears into it, it's not getting you anywhere. It's not really worth it. It's just a matter of what happens.

DANNY SANCHEZ took the experience he gained in the streets after realizing that he had the skills, the heart, and the desire to compete, and he channeled it into boxing. He was very successful as an amateur, but shortly before becoming a professional, he was in a car accident that derailed his plans. He later became a successful photographer with his own studio. He still spars at a local boxing club and helps teenagers learn boxing.

We lived in a poor, bad neighborhood, upstairs from a bar, where there were fights and stabbings all the time. I guess it was the New Jersey version of a redneck town with a bad element. People don't have much, and I guess that's what you end up with. But the people that you hang out with and get in fights with and get in trouble with really become your family in a sense, because you look for them every day and that's what you deal with all the time.

Fighting is your life. I mean, you don't have anything else, so it's what you do. The only thing you have is a reputation for being a tough guy. You don't have money to do anything to make yourself. There's just nothing else. It's not like those other kids who go boating with their dads and stuff like that. Their lives would be occupied with other things rather than just hanging around and getting in trouble.

It was something you had to deal with, and even if it was out of fear and the situation worked out well for you, then it was a good feeling. So I can see you liking the results and the attention you got. If you got into a scuffle as a kid, all the guys who hung out at the bars would come out and see the fight going on and they would say, "Oh, he's a tough kid. Don't mess with him, boy." When you get that kind of recognition and that kind of attention, even girls would like you, you know. And you build that reputation of being a fighter and being somebody not to mess with. So, if you were out on the street and living in a bad neighborhood, fighting was an important thing. And it was rare that somebody, some kid in the neighborhood, would get away without having a fight.

Once I started boxing, I never got into a street fight. Never. It was more of a social thing, I think, the street fighting. There was a social aspect to it. It was how people viewed you in the neighborhood. As a boxer, you don't give a shit about any of that. Now you're more self-contained, you have more respect for yourself, you have nothing to hide. You have a little more pride in what you're doing. To beat somebody up in a bar or on the street, or to hit somebody on the head with a two-by-four on the street, is fine for the moment. You survived it, you lived it, you came out on top in what you had to do, but when you're back in your room, you may not be feeling that great about life in general and there's nothing really that positive about it.

COLE MILLER

is an MMA fighter currently fighting in the featherweight class in the Ultimate Fighting Championship. He trains at American Top Team and received a brown belt in Brazilian jiu jitsu from Ricardo Liborio. Cole was a contestant on The Ultimate Fighter 5 show.

Losing is a big deal to a lot of people for various reasons. Some people are very competitive. They grow up in a competitive atmosphere, whether because of family or an overbearing father who pushes them. Losing itself can consume or haunt an individual, but for me it's not about the winning or losing; it's really about fighting—that's what I want. I really enjoy the fight. I like the adversity, overcoming the agony. I want someone to hurt me so I can reach down deep, find out some things about myself as a person and as a fighter, and elevate myself to that next level. I want somebody to bring out the best in me.

And that's why I fight. I really enjoy that struggle, so when I lose there is something that sticks out about the loss. It's never the loss itself. I played baseball in college. If you strike out once in three times at bat and get two hits, you're pretty successful. But in team sports like that, you lose all the time because of other people, or because your guys didn't work well as a group. I never really played a sport where everything was riding on me. I didn't wrestle in high school. I didn't do martial arts growing up or other competitive sports where it's all you.

Some people don't realize that mixed martial artists are different from fighters. Martial "arts"—that's the key word but a lot of people leave it out. I have a lot of pride and integrity in what I do, and I'm very passionate about my work. You don't just learn a series of techniques. You find the techniques that work for you, and you fight with a certain style, a certain type of aggression. Some people sit back and are elusive; some are counter-fighters; some are balls to the walls in attacking fighters. So it is an art. When I didn't put myself into it, I lost a lot of self-respect, and that changed me. I needed to move, to change scenery. So I decided I might as well go train with the best. At the time the American Top Team was all the rage, and that was where everything was going on with the teams, so I moved there.

My dream was to fight in a Shooto match, and I got my chance when the Shooto organization in Japan was looking for someone to fight Takeshi Inoue, the champion, in a non-titled bout. I found out about it eight days before the fight. I had no money and had to scramble to get money to expedite a passport. So I fought the world champ, and we went all three rounds. He was 8 or 9 and 1 as a pro at the time and a blue belt in jiu jitsu. Because I came from the American Top Team, they thought I was a ground guy, and when they heard "blue belt," they said "perfect." I gave it everything I had and it was a very competitive fight; I felt that I won the first two rounds. It changed me a lot. Here was a champ at 143 pounds, and I could compete with him. For a 145-pounder, that was as big as it got.

Being on the *Ultimate Fighter* show was also huge for me. After the Shooto match, I got an opportunity to fight in Virginia, where Joe Silva, the matchmaker for the UFC, was from. He came to a local event I was fighting in and told me he liked my style. Technically I wasn't complete yet, but he liked what I brought to the table, my fighting spirit. We kept in touch and he put in a good word with the show, so I went to the tryout and the producers liked me. Being on Ultimate Fighter did exactly what I wanted it to do; it gave me a gateway into the UFC and proved I belonged there with those elite fighters. I was able to test myself as an individual and as a fighter. I got to meet some good people, some I still keep in touch with, and it changed me a lot.

RAMIL ABREAU

was a high school student who did clerical work for three hours after school, trained as a boxer for three more hours five days a week, and then completed her homework. She decided to become a pro boxer when she became eighteen. As an amateur boxer, Ramil won eighteen of her twenty bouts.

I know that both opponents train, but in the ring is where you see who wants it more. Who really trained harder for this? The one who doesn't give up. You have to throw in there, push yourself until you feel like you're going to die. Until you feel like you can't take it anymore, like you're going to pass out. That's what you have to think. At least that's how I've been trained. You have to throw and keep on punching, be like a gear on a bicycle, and when you see yourself stopping, you have to keep on pedaling; you have to keep on coming. That's the thing you have to do.

In a bout, you got to keep going, like you have to keep going. You have to tell yourself in your mind: "Come on! You got to do it! You can do it if you want!" They always think there's a limit, when *you* can still keep on going more. Even me, sometimes I have felt like that. But my coach starts yelling, like a typical regular coach starts yelling. He gets frustrated, he gets mad. And when he tells me that, I get even angrier. I get mad and I just go in there and throw hard punches. I just get mad. Even though he tells me, you got to know how to manage everything, control it 'cause you can't go in

there mad. 'Cause you're just going to throw yourself off. You're gonna throw punches just to kill them, and you're not gonna really like look professional, you know.

I fought in Florida last summer and I fought with anger. I was mad at my coach for some reason, and I went in the ring mad at him. And I regret that, you know? 'Cause even though I won both of the fights that I fought there, I think I could have done way better than that if I had my mind focused and if I hadn't been as mad as I was.

I can take a punch and I've gotten hit hard. Yesterday I was sparring, and I was like: "Steve [my trainer], I don't want to put no headgear on today, 'cause I'm trying to turn pro soon, so I want to get kind of used to it." And I sparred with a guy I had knocked out before. Now he was better, he'd gotten better. We just go at it every time we spar. And he went in without the headgear too. As we were turning, we head-bumped each other. And we both stopped because I saw something blank, I saw blank. I couldn't see completely, and he couldn't either. And I was like, this hurts more without headgear than with the headgear. It feels so much different.

BILL SCOTT was a three-times Regional and District Champ in high school with a 96–9–1 record. In college he was 77–4 as a wrestler and attained All-American status. He is a 1st degree Brazilian jiu jitsu black belt and has competed in grappling and professional mixed martial arts events. He is a full time jiu jitsu instructor.

After wrestling, there really was nothing other than Pro Wrestling, I'm old. Not that old, but old for the sport. Not jiu jitsu, but MMA fighting. I just turned forty-one, and I'm probably in the ten percent of the guys my age that are able to still compete. And my whole thing was, I did it to stay in shape. When I first started, I was like, "Let me do something to get back into shape."

It's weird, you know. I'm not saying I like to get hit, but it doesn't bother me. And that was the first thing I had to overcome when I started training for no rules—getting hit. The first thing was shying away from getting hit, like turning away. And now it's just something that I overcame after I got hit a few times. You start getting used to it. Some people never get used to it and they don't do well in the fights. You'll see them do a couple fights, and that's it. It's the wrong sport, you know? But some guys feed on that. You get hit a few times, and it gets your blood pumping. It's addictive.

OLEG SAVITSKY

was born in Georgia, USSR, and began Greco-Roman wrestling training at the age of eight. He also trained in free-style wrestling, boxing, and Sambo. He was trained by top combat experts from Russian Special Operations Units. He and his family immigrated to the United States and became citizens. He competed in sambo and MMA and later opened his own training school, Zealous Nation, in New Jersey, where he trains amateur and professional MMA fighters.

I am very proud to be an American citizen, and I'm very proud of the fact that my knowledge and expertise have helped me to earn medals for this great country. I have competed many times in the world championships in Combat Sambo, and when I reached the top of the podium representing the United States, I was very, very happy about that.

I participated in the first world championships in Combat Sambo in 2001 in the south of France, and it was a very tough competition. The rules are that if you knock out the guy twice, you win the fight. I did it four times, and because it was the first world championship, I had to fight in the finals with the guy who represented Russia. Sambo is a Russian national sport, so it was going to be impossible for an American to win the first world combat championship and take it away from the Russians. I don't like to make excuses, but I have it documented in newspaper articles that they did a lot of tricks over there and I lost. The audience was disgusted and they were booing. I thought it was funny that the French actually supported the Americans; they were rooting for Americans. I was so upset because it was the first time that I got so badly judged, but then I realized what was going on—it was a political thing.

Next time, in 2002, I made it all the way to the finals again, representing the United States, and I was fighting in an absolute division, which means that there are no weight restrictions. In the finals, I had to face a guy I knew already, a professional fighter who was very promising. He did extremely well in Pride, which at that time was a not very well known tournament in the United States. His name was Fedor Emelianko. One of the guys on my team, Don Fernett, asked if I knew who I was going to fight. "I just saw this guy," he said to me. "He destroyed Semmy Schilt, a gigantic fighter, the best striker and a K1 World GP champion." And I had to face Fedor in the absolute division finals. I lost on points, because he was able to throw me a few times. Very powerful, unbelievable technique, very quick hands. But to a certain degree, it was funny, because the guys who represent Russia told me, "Oh, he fights kind of the same style as you. So it's going to be a beautiful finals." And it was, the first time I faced Fedor.

My good background in boxing helped me a lot when I faced him a second time, which was the semi-finals in Prague in 2005. Again I lost to him on points, but it was an interesting fight. Fighting a guy like him is not only a privilege but it's a great experience. And we developed a very nice relationship. He's one of the humblest and toughest guys I ever met in my life. It's a very interesting experience to meet somebody like this who is well rounded, very religious, extremely well read, and very knowledgeable. He's the kindest person you want to meet, and he never sees himself as a star, but at the same time, he is the most dangerous guy on the planet. One of the things that makes me relate to him is he doesn't let his anger or passion show. He is in the cage or the ring and he fights his opponents because that's his job. But at the same time he has no resentment toward them. He understands that's the way they earn their bread and he never says anything bad about anybody. Knowing somebody like that teaches you a lot and gives you an opportunity to learn how to control your anger, your fear, your anxieties. Because of that experience, I never feel any resentment toward my opponents when I'm fighting.

FRANCISCO MANSUR is a Grand Master (red belt) in Brazilian jiu jitsu. He trained under Helio Gracie, who awarded all of his belts. Francisco was a police chief in Rio de Janeiro and has a degree in law. He won 38 of 39 vale tudo fights in Brazil, with one draw. He is the author of more than forty books on jiu jitsu.

I began training in jiu jitsu when I was fifteen years old, which means that I have trained in jiu jitsu for fifty-five years of my life. My instructor, my master, my second father is Helio Gracie, who was my first and only instructor. I trained in all the martial arts—judo, karate, boxing, Kung fu. All my life I trained in fighting, but nothing is the same as jiu jitsu. Brazilian jiu jitsu is a special fight system, and it will change your life.

I have always been involved with violence. I was a police officer in Brazil for thirty-five years, and all my life I have fought organized crime, which was very strong in Brazil, especially in drugs. Now it is better, but in my time it was different. Eleven times I got shot in combat by the bad guys, but jiu jitsu helped me to survive. God saved my life a lot of times, and jiu jitsu helped.

EDIENE "INDIO" GOMES is from Sao Paulo, Brazil. She is a black belt in Brazilian jiu jitsu and has been an MMA fighter since 2007. She fights as a featherweight (146 pounds).

When I was young, I was a little troublemaker in the streets, so I decided to go to a gym in the city. I started jiu jitsu first at thirteen, and I fell in love and never stopped. But what happened was that with jiu jitsu, you go for tournaments and you just fight for medals. It is hard to make a living with only jiu jitsu. When I started getting really tough with jiu jitsu, I decided to move to MMA to make some money to start paying bills. I went to a lot of tournaments, got my black belt, went to a world championship and finished in second place, a silver medal. I got a little disappointed with jiu jitsu because I got a lot of bad calls with the referees. When the referees made a bad decision, I got frustrated with the whole thing. I decided that I would stop fighting in jiu jitsu because I would never make money, and I decided to move to MMA. And at every single jiu jitsu tournament I go to, the referee does something, makes bad calls.

I fought against a guy in my second MMA fight in Brazil. One of my friends called me and said, "I have a fight next month. Do you want to take it?" I said, "Yeah, sure," but my friend didn't mention that I would be fighting a guy. I started training. When I showed up, it was a guy. I took the fight and I kicked the guy's ass. Right after this, I had trouble finding a fight against another girl because a lot of girls looked at me like, "She's that girl who kicked a guy's ass." A lot of girls look at me like I fought a guy already, so they don't want to take this fight. I took the fight on that day with the guy because I had to fight and money was tight.

Altogether, I fought seven MMA fights in Brazil. Five of the fights I won by submission and one by knockout. One I lost because I had to drop a lot of weight and fight at 135, which is not my division.

After I moved to Florida, I scheduled eight fights, and all of the girls canceled. I am still having a hard time finding fights. Two weeks ago, I fought in Jacksonville and I won by submission. I got an armbar.

Usually, this sport is more for guys. At this gym, like any other gym, it is ninety-nine percent guys. I have no choice, but I have to train against guys. I do really well against guys. I got used to this because I am training with guys, and I am not scared and I'm on the same level with the guys. When a new girl comes to train here, they get scared because I train with guys and look tough. They complain they hurt this or they hurt that. I like training with guys because the guys never complain.

I'm still training hard. I'm a full-time fighter. I train every single day. I'm waiting to get some connections, like Strikeforce, because they have a lot of girls there. I really want to go to the Strikeforce show, because there's a lot of tough girls there. My manager is still working, still talking. I'm waiting and hoping. I want to get a chance to fight against one the best in the world. One of the best in the world right now is Cris Cyborg; she's a champ. If I had a chance against her, I would be more than happy and ready to go. I'm not scared, I'm eager to fight. I want to be the champion.

THIAGO "THE PITBULL" ALVES is a Brazilian professional

MMA fighter who competes in the UFC's welterweight division. Thiago began training in Muay Thai in Brazil and competed in it as a teenager. He has a brown belt in Brazilian jiu jitsu.

I got into fighting because I always wanted to fight. I had always watched fighting movies, with Bruce Lee and Van Damme and all those Chinese and Japanese ninjas. At seven years old, I studied karate and after that some capoeira. At thirteen, I started concentrating on Muay Thai, and at fifteen I had my first amateur fight in Muay Thai. It was a tournament, and I won two fights in one night. I fought for a few years as an amateur and had my first professional fight when I was seventeen.

I always had a talent for fighting and martial arts. I pick up stuff really quickly and I love what I do. That has a lot to do with my becoming a professional. I did twenty-one fights in Brazil. My first five fights were bare knuckles with no rules, and you could do whatever you want. I lost my first fight, but after that I never lost one. I was the youngest guy in the gym through my whole training in Brazil. In my first professional Muay Thai fight, I was just fifteen and the other guy was twenty-five. I usually fought people much older than me. I used to fight at about 175 pounds, but most of the time the other people were heavier. I was just having fun. I just wanted to get in there and trade some punches and see how much I had learned. Right now, it is my job, and I know exactly what I've got to do. It's still fun and I still love it, but back then there was no pressure.

It's normal and it's good to have the butterflies before you go into the cage. It keeps you sharp and mentally prepared. If you don't have those butterflies, something is wrong with you. Maybe you didn't have a good day, maybe you don't want to do this anymore. I always get the butterflies, and I love them. As soon as you go out there, everything goes on automatic pilot. You do what you've got to do. You just have to go there and perform. When you care about something and you want to do it right, you get those butterflies.

Walking out for a fight is much more exciting than you think. You compose yourself because you are about to perform and go to the war. We feel like adrenaline junkies when it comes to that. That's why we want go back there and be more prepared and get better and better. At least that's myself, because I love the feeling when you walk into the cage and you know you are prepared. You have that guy in front of you who trained hard too, and you are about to exchange punches and knees and everything that you know, and see who's the better fighter. That's priceless. I really see myself as a gladiator in the modern days; that's how I see UFC fighters, ultimate fighters. There's nothing better than to walk in that tunnel and everybody's screaming. You definitely feel like you've made it.

People have to realize that we are athletes and that nobody else does what we do when it comes to fighting. We are warriors out there, but it's a job. Fighters are very driven people who know what they want and they go after it. We are not scared to do whatever it takes to accomplish what we want. That's what people need to know about us. We're not civilians. We're not normal people. We're athletes. So we can't do what normal people do. I do think we are the sweetest people in the world. It takes a lot for me to get really mad; in fact, I can't remember the last time I was upset. All our issues we just take out in training. Outside of that, we just want to have fun and chill and enjoy. People say all the time that I'm two people. "As soon as you walk in the cage, you're the 'Pitbull' but outside it you're Thiago." Each time I fight, I switch that. I turn it on and I turn it off.

I truly believe that we are the most complete athletes out there because we use all aspects of the body. Your body has to be prepared to move, to wait, to jump when you're not expecting. You've got to be strong with all the speed, all the skills, and your mind has got to be on the same frequency. I know that nobody trains as hard as we do. It's not just a job that we do during the week, it's a 24/7 job, but you have to rest, too. Sometimes people overtrain because they don't rest enough and burn themselves out before the day they have to peak. You have got to have good people around you, a physical therapist and a strength and conditioning coach. They will tell you what to do and how to act, and you've got to trust them. We worry about what we eat, how much water we drink. You can't do this, you can't do that, you've got to rest because you have to train the next day. I think that our lifestyle takes a lot out of us, but we do it because it's what we love, so it's effortless.

BIG ANT is trained in karate and competed in full contact events. He was one of the stars of the reality show Rescue Ink.

When you're growing up in Brooklyn, everything's done on the streets, and so I went to study Tae Kwon Do to learn a form of fighting. I happened to have a very hard core teacher, and he taught us about life. He was half Asian and a really good teacher. He taught the real battlefield kind of thing. We had tournaments, which were school on school. I noticed that the fighters at these schools learned how to do their moves, and they perfected the moves, and then went to the next level. When you knew a move, you would use it in a competition against another school. You actually used it, not just throwing punches in the air and saying, "I won!" It was full contact. Our teacher taught us the real way, that every shot had to be effective.

In some of these fights, these guys fight for a half-hour. Who's got time for that? You just sit there and wait for your shot. You're aggressive. You get it. When your shot is there, you throw your shot out and the fight is over. And that's how he taught us. Just make every shot count. I went by that in my whole life, and that's the way it is. You can see in the street, where you watch guys fighting for two days out there. Who's got time to fight for two days? They've got other stuff to do, you know?

I always stuck to what the teacher said and it was over fast, because the shot counted. You get in, it counts, and that's it. When you're right, you're right and you stand up for your rightness, have respect for everybody and everything, from animals to humans. That's how I was brought up and that's how I did stuff; it always works out. And that's how I live. For instance, I don't hunt. Why am I going to shoot something that can't shoot me back? What's the sport of that?

We used to have fights about once a month, and as soon as we got ready, another school would come in, and that's how we progressed. Everybody's different, so whatever you see that looks effective, that's where you go.

The boxing I do is not professional, just backyard stuff.

I was in a bar with a friend, and the guys there were picking on a guy who had too much to drink. They were picking on him, pushing him this way and that. So we said, "Hey, listen, take it easy. The guy's drunk. He's had too much to drink." So they told us that maybe we should take it outside. And we did, but unfortunately we didn't realize that they were having some kind of party in the bar, and the whole bar was them. We went outside, and so did the whole bar, but we just stood our ground. Everybody was trying to get a shot in and they ended up hitting each other! Everybody was so aggressive; just running into the pack and throwing a fist without thinking where that fist was going to land. They were hitting their friends. They just figured, "Let me throw a fist!"

Karate isn't a hundred percent safe. It's good to have the skill, but, like I said, you've got to be right on. You've got to make every shot count, and if you make every shot count, you're not going to have a problem. It's kind of programmed in you, so you're blocking and you're doing your karate, but you don't want to be there doing karate for four hours. You have to make it effective. You've got to do what you've got to do. But you've got to go home!

TOMMY GUNS, an undefeated underground fighter who survived thirty-five bouts, has a natural athleticism and speed, and he knew from childhood that he was good at fighting. He studied a multitude of martial arts but was never concerned about his ranking in any of them. He took knowledge from each one to use in his fighting.

I started out with judo and karate, and I learned stuff from home boxing. I moved around a lot in my life and never stayed in any one school. I learned many different styles, but the basics were jiu jitsu and Kung fu, which I learned from my friend in Florida, and American karate, which I learned from overseas. If I was driving my car and if guys got out and did something, I wouldn't get steamed up. I would say okay, this is what you're asking for. I tried not to hurt people, but if they were knocking on the door ...

When I was young, I moved to a little redneck town in Florida, because all the schools in NYC kicked me out and there was nowhere left for me to go. I met a kid from Laos and we both drew dragons in class. I would draw my style of dragon and he would draw his culture's dragon, and we became friends through drawing. I had a New York accent and was learning Floridian; he was learning English, and we started doing stuff after school together. We started playing, throwing punches, and kicking, and the next thing you know we took it to the next level and started training. We enjoyed it; that was our fun. When he was a little boy, everybody loved martial arts; it was part of their religion. All of his moves were to kill, not to block, like in America. He was like, "Don't waste time. Get it over with." There was no showboating. He was about fast timing and getting it done. I picked up on it right away, because it came natural. We would do sit ups and push-ups, punch bean bags nailed into palm trees. We would beat them until our hands couldn't even move. We thought that's what everybody did.

One day we were out on a back road coming back from a movie. We both had long hair, and this pickup truck pulled up and they started making comments about us. We didn't know why, but maybe it was because we both have darker skin and dark hair. My friend put his hand out and rolled his fingers back and said: "Come, come, I will show you." Next thing they came out and they were on the ground. They definitely had alcohol on them. I don't think the guy behind the wheel ever got out of the vehicle, but there were at least three others. I remember they came toward us; the first thing was the kicks and then they were on the ground, and the next thing we were punching their faces. Taking them out was simple. We were kind of shocked that it was happening, but we were like, "Wow, we finally got to do it." I said to my friend that we might as well count this as part of the day's training, part of the sparring. That was our play time. We were half their size, about fifteen years old. This happened many times, the racial card, with him being Asian. People weren't accustomed to it. With him and without him, I have had a lot of episodes of nonsense with people. But I was never a bully, never one for starting it, or even looking for it. I used to have a crazy, dark cloud of idiots that found me.

Someone told me about underground fights, where there would be some money and where everything will be fine, there wouldn't be any guns or knives. You throw a couple of punches and see how it goes from there. And when you're there, you realize that it's more than that. It was different then from what it is today. Today everything is a brand name. Back then it was training, or you could make a couple of bucks doing something. I traveled from state to state doing underground fights. The fights took place at gyms after hours, basements, outside, or even an old hangar. I did it from high school for a couple of years until my son was born, then I stopped. I came back. I was doing anything just to make a buck.

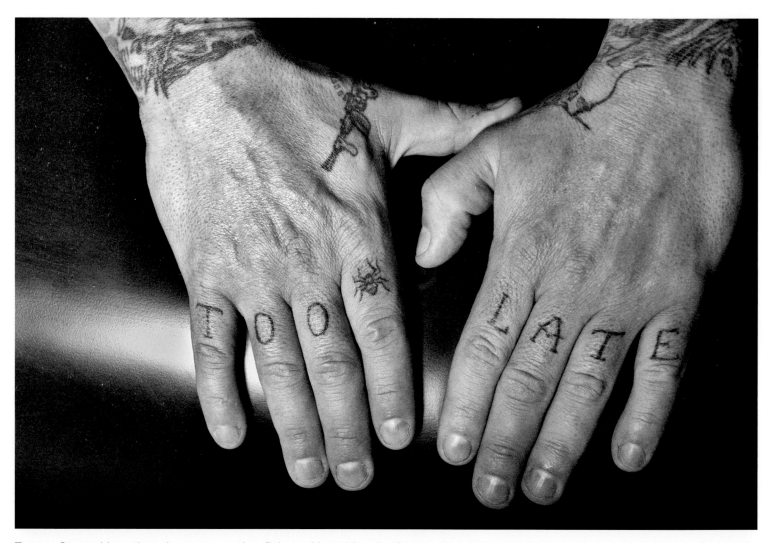

Tommy Guns told me that when someone in a fight could read "too late" tattooed on his hands, it was too late. I saw evidence of this while we were talking: he demonstrated incredible control and speed when he unexpectedly swung at my eye and stopped the punch within a half inch of my eye. Even though I was facing him, it happened so quickly that I did not see it coming and there would not have been enough time for me to move out of the way.

In my fights, when one person was standing and the other was lying on the ground, that was it. There was no referee, so it depended on how far each person took it. If someone was down on the ground, I didn't want to kick their teeth in, or break them up and act like an asshole. If I seen they were done, I was done. It wasn't about hurting; it was about showing your skills and moving on. I wasn't one to make examples and look for showboating. I'd rather just tap them, get them down, and that was it. They were out of breath, and I'd go back to the car and leave. There were no weapons, they didn't want anybody to have any kind of salt, or any kind of stuff like that to blow in the eyes, or any kind of magic tricks. They would definitely have somebody make sure that you weren't carrying a piece of steel in your hand, or quarters. There were no rounds, no time-outs, no water. Some of the fights, for me, didn't last that long, anyway. I've never lost, I've never been on the ground, and I've never lost consciousness, still to this day.

We didn't have weight classes. I always kept myself off season at 230 pounds and in season between 210 and 220. I fought all kinds: small, medium, heavy, light. I fought people who were 300 or 400 pounds. They had no steam; they hit hard, but if you can take a punch, it didn't matter. If I saw them looking zany, I would maybe punch them between their bicep and their shoulder, so I know that I could break their arm. I would go for the throat or for the eyes so they couldn't see. It depends on what I'm fighting. It depends on where their feet are and their hands. With wrestlers, their shoulders are a little bit more round as they come toward you. Boxers are a little bit more straight, but then there's the unpredictable, the wild one. Some guys were pretty awesome. I don't think that anybody in these levels were just boxers; I know a lot of them wrestled in school. I know a lot of them learned martial arts. I didn't approach anybody. People started coming up to me. Certain tough guys knew that you could be a shark. Either way, they knew they would make money on me.

I would see how they were handling themselves, or see what hand they were using to pick up something to drink. Or I would see how they were breathing, or even how they were looking at other people. I would see how focused they were. I would see if they were smoking cigarettes, or doing whatever, from a distance, just watching to see what I was dealing with. The unpredictable was the hardest, but if you knew someone who was smoking cigarettes, or if their friends were a little different, they were the bar type and you knew that the guy was just going to come at you. If you had people who were reading the Bible and being quiet, then you said to yourself, "I've got something to deal with." No one wore gloves, maybe taped hands. Guys wore jeans. There were no fancy sweat pants. You didn't want to look like a fighter.

There was one time I fought someone older than me. He had fought in the Navy and was no slouch; he was definitely a tough man. I was new to underground fighting, but I was not new to fighting. I sort of liked the guy and we went at it, and he punched me really hard. He rocked my bell. I got him down and twisted his foot and broke it. After I was done, I put my hand out and I said to him, "You know, you are a great fighter. I'm sorry I did that to you." I gave him all respect. I picked him up. I said no one ever hit me like that before. I was really thankful. He had the eye of proudness because I didn't act like I was better than him and I was honored to be there. He had the biggest smile on his face. I made his day. I let him know that he was the best and I got lucky.

JOHN MOLNAR

JOHN MOLNAR was a Golden Glove champ three times as an amateur boxer and became a pro one month before his twenty-third birthday. As a pro welterweight, he compiled a record of twenty wins (forty-seven percent by KO), two draws, and two losses. A recurrent shoulder injury that required numerous surgeries ended his career.

I remember way back when I was watching boxing with my dad and Uncle Bill. It was always interesting, and I said that I can do this. My parents said they bought me boxing gloves when I was three years old. When I was fifteen, they told me that if I could get my grades up and stay out of trouble, I could go to the gym and learn how to box. My first fight was when I was sixteen. It was in a warehouse in Jersey City. There was smoke all over, beer everywhere. It was weird. I said to my trainer that there was something different about my opponent. He said, "Yeah, he's a leftie." I was so nervous I didn't notice that he was a leftie, but I won.

I won the Golden Gloves three times, and I won the State Championship ABF four times. Altogether I had twelve or thirteen amateur titles. I loved it. I was twenty-two when I turned pro. My manager, Pete Finn, who had been my trainer originally, saw me coming in every day and saw how dedicated I was. So he started to work with me exclusively, just me every day. He is still a good friend. I was best man at his wedding and he was in mine. He hooked up with Pat Lynch, who was Arturo Gatti's manager, and they did a co-management deal, so I sparred regularly with Gatti, probably about two thousand rounds.

It takes a special person to go into the ring, to get hit, keep on coming, and then come back the next day and say, "Okay, we have to spar again." It's very rare. I have talked with a few guys at the gym, friends of mine who were football players, big guys. After sparring, that's it, they're done; they never want to do it again, never want to box again. They can play football and break bones, but they can't take a punch in the face. It's a different game. Some people think that you have to be stupid to fight, but boxing is like a big chess game. It's a thinking man's game. People don't realize that; they think that you just have to be strong to box.

I used to take a shot to give a shot. I won't say I was the fastest guy in the world, but I could take it. You could hit me once, you could hit me twice, but I would get a good shot on you. I didn't have the best defense in the world. It was weird, because sometimes I could do it and sometimes I wouldn't do it. So then I would just be a bull, try to move and just hit. I don't mind taking a shot, or two, or five.

I never got knocked out. They stopped one fight in Atlantic City that was on ESPN. I got knocked down in the first round and I tore my shoulder, the tendon in my shoulder, but I went nine more rounds. I had a cut under one eye, my eyes were swollen, and they stopped it with about twenty seconds left in the ninth round. I was aggravated that they stopped it. I said, "Let me finish the fight." The ref was like, "No, you took enough." I said, "Wait a minute! For nine rounds you let me get my ass kicked, and now you're worried about me not having enough in the last round. C'mon!" I was aggravated because I wasn't hurt at all. They were worried about me because I had one arm, two swollen eyes, a cut under one eye, and they knew I wasn't going to stop. I said, "I can finish the fight." I didn't think it was that bad.

The shoulder injury came from overtraining, punching hard and missing. That's what stopped my career. I had four surgeries on the shoulder; they would go in arthroscopically and cut it down. The tendon would heal itself because it was not cut down completely. I would need surgery every ten fights, and then five fights, and then one fight. I couldn't do it anymore. I had a wife and kid.

GENE LEBELL is a former professional wrestler, boxer, and judo champ. He is a 10th-degree red belt in judo and a 9th-degree black belt in jiu jitsu. He has worked as a stuntman in more than 1,000 films and television shows, and he still does so. Gene is the author of numerous martial arts books and is also a trainer, teacher, and referee. In 1963, Gene won the first televised mixed martial arts event by choking fifth-ranked professional light heavyweight boxer Milo Savage. Gene is called the Godfather of Grappling, Judo Gene, and the Toughest Man Alive.

For thirty-eight years, my mother, Aileen Eaton, ran a boxing and wrestling auditorium in Los Angeles that had been built for the 1932 Olympics. When I was seven, after my father passed away, she was a single parent and wanted to get rid of me, so she sent me down to the L.A. Athletic Club, where professional wrestlers and boxers trained. I got a chance to work out with the top wrestlers in the world of that time. They were all men and I was a kid. They taught me grappling, which I spent the rest of my life doing, what we now know is a combination of all the martial arts. I got to train at the Main Street Gym downtown, where professional boxers, including Sugar Ray Robinson, trained. I got a chance to spar with him when I was a kid. He was a world champion and he enjoyed showing me that he was the best of all time.

When I was a kid at the boxing gym, somebody started beating me up because he was bigger, older, and tougher. I would pick him up and body slam him, and they would kick me out of the gym for a couple of days. In the wrestling gym, somebody who was bigger, stronger, tougher than me would beat me up a little bit, and I'd knock him out with a left hook or an uppercut. So I would get kicked out of that gym also.

The harder you work, the luckier you get. You can always tell how hard a person in the ring has worked. If he wins, they say, "Oh he had an easy fight." But, they don't think about the hundreds of hours that he spends in the gym and doing roadwork and exercise and calisthenics to get in shape to become a winner in the ring.

I won a lot of trophies beating up tough guys. If you put all the trophies together, they wouldn't buy a car, they don't add up to one house payment. But I've been to Mecca and I played with the gods. But you can't eat those trophies, you can't eat glory, you can't eat those handshakes. You can't cash them at the bank.

Let me tell you what is good about the martial arts, how it's changed my life. I competed in the service, and after I came out, I wrestled professionally, when I got a chance to do a little in the movies and became a stuntman. I'm in a group called Stunts Unlimited, along with fifty of the top stunt people in the world. Put it this way: every star in Hollywood has beaten me up, including Jack Benny, John Wayne, and many more. I'm usually the villain. I like to say that every star, man or woman, has beaten me up at one time or another. No trophies, but now I'm a millionaire. I have thirty-five motorcycles, a fistful of cars, and a ranch, all paid from losing. That's from the martial arts because they are what got me into being a stuntman in the movies.

When I teach at the dojo, I don't try to make money. I teach for free and I help some of these guys who would ordinarily be hoodlums or lazy bums. Anybody who doesn't give respect, he's out of the gym, or we give him what we call an "attitude adjustment." And you can just imagine in your worst nightmare what that is. In a gym like that, you can beat up a guy and it is perfectly legal. They either quit, or they come back and their attitude is changed.

MAD DOG (Joe Latempa) is a professional wrestler, bouncer, and bounty hunter.

My name is "Mad Dog" Joe. That's my real name. My uncle was a professional wrestler, and I had wanted to become a professional wrestler since I was four years old. Now I'm thirty-one, seventeen years into the business. I've held sixteen world titles, four tag team titles, and sixty-nine state titles. I fought the greatest guys in the business, like the Honky-Tonk Magic, the (Snake) Roberts, King Kong Bundy, Bam Bam Bigello, a lot of the professionals, a lot of the 1980s guys, the legends. I'd rather work with the legends, because you know you're gonna come out of a match not hurt. The guys now are so brutal. They know you've been in the business and they try to take you out of the business, knowing that you have bad knees, arthritis, and stuff like that. They have no morals and no sorrows. They want to be number one.

So now I'm a bouncer, which I love. I work in a go-go bar. What's better than working in a go-go bar? You sit down and watch women dance. Basically, I'm a calm guy, a cooler. I don't like to start fights. I calm the guys down. But if they ask to get physical, I gotta get down and dirty.

And then there's bounty hunting, where I go out and catch fugitives that jump bail, the most dangerous job out there, because you don't know who you're going after and you don't know who's gonna shoot at you or who's gonna stab you. They will call me up and say, "We've got to catch this fugitive. He's armed and dangerous." Now what do you do? You go out there with a team of four and catch the guy. There are two things you can do. You can pepper spray him or you can take a baton, hit him on the back of the leg, let him go down, and then hold him down until we can cuff him and throw him into the car. I've been shot at; I've been stabbed. Four hundred pounds, six feet tall, but it doesn't mean anything. You got a little guy out there that's nuts, crazy as hell; he'll do anything just to try to get you down. But that's why I have the special wrestling skills.

And it's a great job for me. I got the size, the ability, the skills. And I've got the mind for it. Some of these guys don't have the mind for it; they want to be gun slayers who do what they have to do to catch a fugitive. But it's not like that; it's all about the mind and the way you grab these guys, the way you treat them. You gotta treat them with respect. If they don't treat you with respect, you can give them a little harm back. But if they've come in nice, then I treat them with respect. And basically, that's the bounty hunting business. It's good money and if it were an everyday thing it would be great money. But bouncing is full-time for me, because my body's all torn up. You know, seventeen years flying around, doing flips at 400 pounds. It hurts the body. But I chose this life. I love living on the edge. I'm doing three things that I always wanted to be: a professional wrestler, a bouncer, and a bounty hunter.

MIKE MEDRANO wrestled in high school. He played football in college and later was a semi-pro. He became a pro mixed martial arts fighter after leaving football. Mike works as a high school social studies teacher.

I got into mixed martial arts to help me get better for football. I used Capoeria, which is a Brazilian art, to help me with my balance, to help me with my stamina, and my stretching. And then from there, football was frustrating. I couldn't get an NFL contract, so I decided to learn jiu jitsu and boxing and Muay Thai and bring it to fighting. So I retired from football to go into fighting, which has been a good experience.

They complement each other. To get powerful and muscular for football, and then to have the endurance for mixed martial arts, it benefitted. So now I'm hitting like I would hit in a football game, but it's more for a longer duration, three five-minute rounds. So I'm using that power consistently in mixed martial arts and some people really are not used to that.

You get forty-five second rests between each play. A running back would get twenty to twenty-five carries a game. That's how much beating you could take in a game. But with mixed martial arts it's three five-minute rounds straight with a minute break. That's a lot of cardio. That's hard cardio. That's why I've lost so much weight. I played running back at 205. I fight at 170. The more muscle you have, the more oxygen you need.

People can't judge you. And that's what frustrated me about football. I could be a thousand-yard rusher and still not be good enough for the Giants or for—I've worked out with the Tampa Bay Bucks and Tampa Bay Storm because I'm only 5'5". I was only weighing two hundred pounds, you know? And you could still be a thousand-yard rusher, be a quality football player, but not fit their scheme because it's just opinion. That coach doesn't like that height or that weight. They'd rather have another one.

But with this (MMA), you prove yourself as a man one on one. Nobody can say anything. You could be 5'5" and still be 10–1, 10–2, which is the plan. I've only lost twice, off of mistakes. It wasn't like I was getting my ass whipped either. They were mental mistakes that were early in my career and you learn from them and become a better fighter.

I'm telling you, there have been a lot of street fights that I have not dominated or won, you know, especially when there is more than one person. You're going to take some lickings. Yeah. There's no referee. I mean, that's what's funny. In MMA, it's one person in a cage. You've got a ref and you got a doctor. What is there to be scared of? And the dude is not heavier than you, and he has no weapons. So, we're okay.

JEFF GRAF is a 1st degree black belt in Michi Budo Ryu and a brown belt in Tae Kwon Do. Twice he was inducted into the Martial Arts Hall of Fame. In the U.S. Army, he was a commander of a military special reaction team and was involved in hostage rescues and various other anti-terrorism situations. His martial arts skills saved his life on various combat missions, and he taught martial arts to SWAT teams and other military personnel. He is now a special agent in the counter-terrorism field and is teaching martial arts to military elite personnel.

GINA REYES is a Muay Thai fighter, a master-level personal trainer, and co-owner of American Boxing in San Diego. She was a kinesiology major at San Diego State and a member of the men's crew team the year they went to the national championships. Four months after beginning Muay Thai training, she won her first match against an experienced opponent. She fought on Team Menor for Melcor Menor, the Muay Thai world champion, and was featured on the Oxygen channel's reality show Fight Girls.

JONAS NUNEZ, JR. is a former South Bronx street gang member who later entered college and majored in business administration. As a boy, he was an amateur boxer and began martial arts training. He obtained a 9th degree black belt in Okinawan Shindo Ryu karate and participated in hundreds of full-contact karate matches and tournaments. He is a former Professional Karate Association champion and owns seven martial arts schools, where he has trained numerous martial arts champions.

JOSE SULSONA

began training in kickboxing and karate as a child in Puerto Rico in order to defend himself in a violent neighborhood. He became the 175-pound kickboxing champion in Puerto Rico. When he moved to New Jersey, he continued to compete in kickboxing. He added jiu jitsu to his skills and competed in mixed martial arts events. Jose is now a kickboxing and karate trainer.

FRANCISCO "MASTER INDIO" PEREIRA DA SILVA

is a legendary vale tudo fighter in Brazil with more than three hundred bouts in which the fighters did not wear gloves or mouth guards. He was trained in judo and received a black belt in Brazilian jiu jitsu from Carlson Gracie.

In 1955, I started at thirteen or fourteen with a Japanese master in judo. In 1957, I started fighting in Brazil on a television show, and then I did about fifty fights. After that, I fought in different promotions in towns where the mayors would put on little shows for people to watch. The government people and the military liked the fights. I started getting bigger and my name was getting popular, so I began fighting in the big shows. I fought in the North and Northeast areas of Brazil almost every week. It used to be really tough, and it was my big dream to go to the Gracie Academy in Rio de Janeiro. After a while, I was able to make it. I got a job in the gym cleaning the mats and was able to train for free. I met Carlson Gracie and we became good friends. We used to train together a lot.

I fought judo and jiu jitsu and vale tudo. I had more than 300 vale tudo matches and probably had sixty percent wins with forty percent losses. It's hard to track, because back in those days they didn't have cameras, especially in Brazil, where they were very expensive. We used to have tournaments between the North and the Northeast to see who were the toughest fighters. I won a couple and lost a couple, too. Back then it used to be ten rounds of ten minutes each, with a minute to rest in between rounds. I was very popular and everyone wanted to have me in the show because I sold a lot of tickets. I fought all of the big names of the day except for Carlson Gracie and Euclides Pereira, because they were very close friends of mine. We used to travel in the back of the truck for two or three days to another city so we could fight again and make some money.

I worked as a bodyguard for the president of Brazil and sometimes I fought while I was working for the government. Sometimes they had to delay the show because the president wanted to see the show and he was late because of work. The president usually watched the fights from ringside and he always encouraged me. I used to be the chief of the whole security team, so I wasn't able to train to fight then. I had to give up my training for the job. Sometimes popes or presidents of other countries would visit. We had to work for a month in advance to take care of the whole security plan and then take care of the person.

I retired thirty-two years ago, but I still teach. I used to have a gym in Brasilia, the capitol of Brazil, and a television show where I taught self-defense to women once a week. God was really good to me. I was always really lucky to have the best professors. They always liked me and took care of me. I thank Carlson Gracie for everything he taught me. I am really happy to pass my legacy and training to my four sons, Marcus, Danillo, Dobles, and Yuri. For my sons to be fighters is my glory.

DANILLO VILLEFORT is the son of the legendary vale tudo fighter Francisco Pereira Da Silva, and he has three brothers who are professional fighters. He is a mixed martial arts fighter who came to America after six matches in Brazil in order to learn how to become well rounded as a fighter. He has a black belt in judo, was on the Brazilian National Team, and was the South American champion.

YURI VILLEFORT is one of four brothers who are all professional fighters. His father is the legendary vale tudo fighter Francisco Pereira Da Silva. Yuri is a brown belt in judo. He is trained in Brazilian jiu jitsu and was the Brazilian champion, as well as a world no gi champion. He became a mixed martial arts fighter when he moved to America.

BRIDGET NARCISSE CHRISTMAN is a mixed martial arts fighter with a B.S. in marketing, who left a career as director of marketing and account executive for an insurance brokerage firm to train full time and pursue her career as a MMA fighter.

I have been training since about 2006. I started just doing kickboxing for fitness, to get into shape after I had my son. I was very thin, at 118 pounds, but now I'm almost 140. My biggest problem is getting warmed up. I don't know if it's mental or physical, but you want to step onto the mat or into the ring and—bing—be on automatic pilot.

I didn't know what to expect getting into this, and I kind of got into it accidentally. I was always a boxing fan as a kid, but my parents said, "No, you don't want to mess your face up like that." I would watch UFC but I didn't know anybody's names or the history of the sports. I just started doing it because I liked it, and one thing led to another. The first time I walked into the karate place, I didn't know what to expect. What kind of people go there? What kind of women do this? But then you start meeting people there and these were my kind of people. They are not only nice, but outgoing, friendly, helpful, respectful. Even my own coach is that way. If he sees someone going into a match without a coach, he'll offer to coach them during the match.

My first fight ever was probably the best experience because I felt like, ready or not, I'm doing this for fun. Who really cares what happens? The worst-case scenario isn't really that bad, so let's go do it. My mind was completely clear, and I guess that's what meditation is supposed to be. Your body just goes. You've been drilled. In the best athletic situation you are on automatic pilot. At first I thought "I don't belong here. These girls know so much more than me. They're going to pull out some kind of magic that I've never seen." But my coach got me through that. He told me, "You know more than them. You're stronger than them. You know more technique. They play a very orchestrated game. They like to jump guard. They like to wait for you to make a mistake. They keep you on the guard, try to armbar, triangle. They're awesome, but it is a very one-dimensional structure that they play in."

I might not be awesome at all those things, but I have a bigger playbook, thanks to this coach. He got me through that, and now I feel fine. I get on the mat and I'm like, "Let's go!" I'm so ready to keep fighting, whether I win or lose. I want to fight again, again, and again. Once you're doing it, you don't want it to end quickly. You want them to submit. Bring more, bring more! My quickest submissions are like twenty-something seconds, from start to finish.

JUSTIN GARCIA grew up in the South Bronx and was involved in many street fights, after which he trained in judo and later wrestling. He has a black belt in Brazilian jiu jitsu and has competed in Abu Dhabi. He is a Grappler's Quest and Superfighting Champion and has fought in mixed martial arts bouts. Justin is a trainer at his own gym, Jungle Gym Martial Arts in the Bronx.

YOSHISADA "YONE" YONEZUKA trained in track and sumo wrestling as a child, studied judo in high school, and was a member of Nihon University's championship judo team. He is a 9th degree black belt in judo and an 8th degree black belt in karate, although when he came to the United States, he was not allowed to compete as an amateur in judo. When he started his own school, he entered full-contact fights against wrestlers and boxers and was undefeated. In 1970, he fought in the National Master's Championship, which he won for seven consecutive years. He has three world championship titles in judo. He also taught judo at West Point and was the Olympic judo coach from 1993 to 1999. He owns the Cranford Judo and Karate Center in New Jersey.

JEFF MONSON

JEFF MONSON wrestled in high school and in Division I competition at Oregon State University. He was a PAC-10 champion. Jeff received a Master's degree in psychology. For years he worked as a mental health professional in a crisis evaluation role and as a child/family counselor. Following graduate school, he began working out at a judo school north of Seattle, which led to a few amateur fights. He won his first match against a kick boxer. "It was almost like an addiction," he said of the career that followed, a career filled with both success and struggle, along with elation and thoughts of self-doubt. Monson is a mixed martial arts fighter, a two-time winner of the ADCC Submission World Championship, and a Brazilian jiu jitsu champion. He fought for and lost the UFC heavyweight championship. In 2012, Jeff won a gold medal at the FILA World Grappling Championship. He also fought in three professional heavyweight boxing matches and had two wins and one draw.

One of the sheiks put on the World Jiu Jitsu Championship. My coach got me in. I was the light heavyweight and I went there and won the tournament, out of literally nowhere. I just moved a lot and kept my good position, and I guess everything followed from there. I was always a-dollar-short kind of thing. I'm really good, but not the elite. I felt great, and after that I had a name.

I remember coming back on the plane and thinking, you know, this demon is off my chest. If I crash right now I could be happy with myself. Of course, that vanished a couple days later when something else came up.

I ended up quitting my job two years later to be a full-time fighter. I had some promises of fights, but they didn't pan out, and all of a sudden I was broke. A guy I knew owned a used car lot in a Hispanic neighborhood and I tried selling cars. I couldn't speak the language, and I needed to get someone else to come in and help me, so, of course, I had to split the commission. I mean, it was the lowest point of my life. I was just so miserable.

I met some guys, went down to Florida, and trained for a week. I stayed in a hotel and had a great time. Got along with the guys really good. They all said, "Hey, do you want to be part of this team we are putting together? We'll give you a monthly stipend. You move down here and you help coach the guys in wrestling because they are jiu jitsu guys and don't know wrestling." My wife wasn't excited about it, but I said, "Man, we're broke, we don't have any money." It's what I wanted to do, and so I went down there.

We were doing two super-hard workouts a day. I wanted to show them they made a good choice, and plus, I was a hard worker.

Then, in practice, I tore by bicep tendon —boom, gone. I had to have surgery and the guy paid for it. I was out nine months. I lost two fights, and now I'm injured. So, it was a bad time.

The best thing that ever happened to me was that injury. I started training correctly. Before, I was overtraining. Constantly, constantly training, wearing my body down, going into fights mentally and

physically fatigued. I changed my schedule and started doing better strength stuff, not the body-building stuff; getting more flexible.

I went on a tear when I got healthy. I won a ton of matches, back in the UFC, back winning in Europe, everything. I was pretty happy and things were going really well, everything kind of fit together. The injury kind of helped me out, put things in perspective.

For the match I lost, the UFC championship, I trained three straight months without fighting. Conditioning three days a week. I was here in the gym and did everything right. I was in good shape. Super good shape. Didn't overtrain. When it came down to the fight, I felt good. I just didn't do the game plan. It's just one of those things where it's mental. I remember going out. They were playing "Imagine" by John Lennon when I was walking out to the ring because I had that as my song. I should have been thinking what I was going to do in the match instead of soaking in the moment.

I had the chance. I remember getting him down in the third round and I had a chance to pass his guard and I didn't pass his guard. I didn't know where I was. I was just living the dream moment and not going, "Screw everything else, screw the crowd, screw my family here and everything else. Just win the match. Just put your nose to the grind and win the match."

I made no excuses, I just didn't do it, and it's just like, you know, for three years now, three and a half years, I've been trying to get back where I have that same opportunity. There are so many guys in our game, you know, who fight for the title and then you never hear from them again. You hear their name—they're fighting here and they're fighting there, but that's it. That was their moment in the sun. They fought for the title. And I don't want to be that guy, you know.

One of my big fears is that somebody is going to call me out. I'm going to be in a gym or something and somebody is going to get everyone's attention and go, "You're not that good. You got lucky. The matches were right, and you won a shot at the UFC championship because this guy wasn't there, that guy wasn't there. And when it came down, you lost and blah, blah, blah. You were just in the right place at the right time. You got lucky. You were never that good. You were too small."

Part of me is like, yeah, maybe they're right. And I don't roll through everybody, you know what I mean? I got guys that I never even heard of give me a rough time, and in my mind I go, "Okay, but in a match I would come out on top." But I don't know, it's just one of those things. I guess it is my own fear, you know. How good am I really?

I want to hear people say champion or former champion. Those words are real because that happened, not like, "You're a legend." But when you say, "Yeah, I won the UFC championship, I won the Strike Force championship," nobody can say that you didn't. No matter what they say about you, that's a fact.

I guess that's what drives me to want to win a title. I can say, "Look I've won a title. At least for today, this day, I'm the best. Or maybe not the best, but I achieved the most I could achieve in this sport today." I can be happy with that.

HOWARD DAVIS, JR. grabbed the attention of Americans in 1976 when he won match after match in the Olympics. His teammates were Sugar Ray Leonard and Michael and Leon Spinks. After the Olympics, Howard became a professional boxer and compiled a record of 36–6–1 with 14 knockouts. He fought for the lightweight title three times against the champions, but did not win. He is currently the boxing instructor at American Top Team, a motivational speaker, and a musician. He also works as a fight promoter with his wife.

Years ago, my father took me to a movie called *A.K.A. Cassius Clay,* a biographical film about Muhammad Ali that came out in 1971. My father ran a gymnasium called Lincoln House in Glen Cove, on Long Island in New York. I was around a lot of boxing, but I was never interested until I saw this movie. I was fifteen years old, which is kind of late to start boxing, but I got so inspired that the next morning I woke up at 4:30 and ran three miles. I trained for five years, won various amateur championships, and went to the Olympics. When I was there, I found out that my mother had passed away and I wanted to go home. But I remembered that her last words to me were, "Good luck ... and you better bring home the gold." Said with a smile on her face. So I stayed and that's what I lived by, every single day of training.

During the Olympics, I got to know Sugar Ray Leonard, the Spinks Brothers, Leo Randolph, Charles Mooney, Davey Armstrong, all those guys. I'd seen them fight, but I never really got to know them up close and personal until we got together as a team. We were all rooting for each other. Sometimes teams can have animosity toward each other, but there was none of that with us. We were very close knit, and I think it showed in terms of winning. We got five gold medals, one silver, and a bronze. At that time, it was the most medals anybody ever won as a team. It was very special.

I read an article once that said, "You're more apt to get struck by lightning than win the Olympics. So when I read that article, I said, "Wow, that puts me as a special category." The older I get, the more I appreciate what we did. Sometimes I think talent is overrated. I worked extremely hard. Talent is one thing and working hard is another. And belief in yourself is another thing, too. I had the talent but I had to work extremely hard at it or I never would have accomplished what I did. And you have to work hard at being lucky, too.

Most of the guys that box come from the ghetto, where the value systems are different. It's about being tough. The value system is about, "if you don't respect me, I'm going to knock you down." I grew up in the ghetto, so I saw it. A lot of kids from the ghetto don't have a mother or a father. I think being a professional fighter teaches respect, but I think most of it comes from your background. I never turn down an autograph, a handshake, or a greeting. That came from my mother and my father—always be humble and always be respectful—never look at yourself as greater than somebody else. I think the most important thing for me is being a decent human being, being honest and forthright. That's it for me.

RAFAEL REBELLO is a 2nd degree black belt in Brazilian jiu jitsu and competes as a bantamweight in mixed martial arts for the World Extreme Cagefighting organization. He owns a gym in Deerfield Beach, Florida, where he trains and coaches students.

JORGE SANTIAGO began practicing karate at the age of six in Brazil. He went on to train in judo and Brazilian jiu jitsu and has a black belt in both disciplines. He won second place in judo at the Pan American Games but is now a mixed martial arts fighter. He fought in the UFC and was the middleweight champion in Strikeforce and Sengoku.

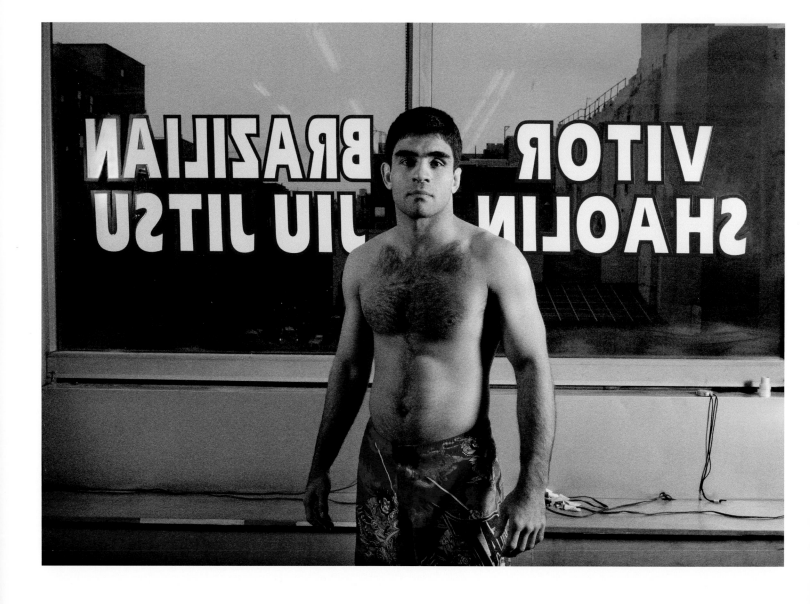

VITOR SHAOLIN RIBIERO is a Brazilian who fought in mixed martial arts for Strikeforce and had a record of 20–5. In MMA he held the Shooto welterweight title and the Cage Rage lightweight championship. He is a 2nd degree black belt in jiu jitsu and won the CBJJ Mundials (world jiu jitsu championship) four times. Vitor owns his own school, Vitor Shaolin Brazilian Jiu Jitsu in Manhattan, where he trains and coaches students.

TOBY GREAR ran track in high school and was the captain of the swim team and co-captain of the football team. In college he competed on the water polo team for two years but decided to look for a new sport and started training in Muay Thai. He realized after earning a degree as a marketing major and working for an advertising firm that his true passion was mixed martial arts, in which he both competed and taught. He is a former two-time Fighting Alliance World Lightweight Champion.

MICHAEL GILLIAM is a 7th degree black belt in American Goshi Shun karate and Tae Kwon Do, a 6th degree black belt in Shotokan karate, a 5th degree black belt in ATA, and a certified Krav Maga instructor. He has also trained in Aikido and Brazilian jiu jitsu. Michael has more than thirty-five years of martial arts experience and has won hundreds of competitions. He is a New Jersey police captain and owns a martial arts school, North Plainfield Fight Club.

I joined the police force in 1988, but I had been a martial arts instructor in the city of Plainfield for about three or four years prior to that. So, a lot of the street guys knew of my reputation. I had won state championships, a lot of world championships, and national championships. When I first got out of the police academy, I was pretty fit, young, and athletic. And I had run track at Rutgers on scholarship, and I was pretty fast. So they put me right in the narcotics bureau and I found myself, six months after graduating from the police academy, dealing with the worst of the worst on the street; guys who would sell drugs to their own mother if they had to. A lot of times I would get out of the car and guys would say, "Oh I know you, you're that karate guy. But that karate stuff doesn't work in the street." I remember when I went to my master, Master Wayne Ford, who I was training with at that time. He said, "Mike, a lot of guys are going to challenge you in the beginning when you are on that police force. But the first person who lays their hands on you has to become such an example that everyone else who is watching will say, 'I'm so glad that wasn't me'."

I remember going to the projects on West Third Street. A guy was reaching into his stash where he was hiding his drugs, and when he turned around, I jumped real fast out of the undercover car we were riding in and surprised the guy. He turned around and dropped the drugs. I told him to put his hands up against the car, that he was under arrest. He said, "I'm not going to jail today." He turned around and started swinging and punching. All I remember were those words from Master Ford. It was the projects, it was a summer day, and everyone was outside. There were a lot of drug dealers on the corner. When we made an arrest in Plainfield at that time, drug dealers would come around and throw bottles and rocks at you while you were trying to arrest the person. So I was like wow, this is probably going to be my opportunity, the one opportunity when people are looking to see what I'll do. I hit this guy hard in his chest and swept him to the ground, and when he tried to get up, I just kneed him in his chest. I kicked him down below and annihilated him, finished him quick. He was one of the tough guys in the project, and when everybody saw how fast that I eliminated that threat, the word went out that I was just an awesome fighter. I started to get a little bit of respect.

BOGDAN GABRIEL CRISTEA is a mixed martial artist from Romania. When he was in Amsterdam, he was hit from behind by a van and left for dead by the driver. He had three surgeries and nearly had his arm amputated, but six months later he resumed his fighting career and knocked out his opponent in four minutes. Bogdan's fight with Daisuke Nakamura is one of the most talked-about fights on YouTube because of his willingness to endure pain when he was caught in numerous jiu jitsu holds, and in all of them he freed himself.

I fell on my shoulder in a fight with a Russian guy, who was a student of Fedor's, in the M1 Challenge Finals. I broke my collarbone in the first round but I didn't realize it. I couldn't move my hand, but I fought another two rounds anyway. He broke it once and then he broke it again; then the piece of the bone in the middle twisted off and my shoulder was swollen. I noticed it in the dressing room, and the doctor said "Man, your collarbone is broken!" I said, "Oh, my God!" I stayed at home for two weeks and didn't take anything for it. The doctor said the bones would heal, but when I went to a specialist, he said, "If you don't get operated on, you cannot fight anymore because your bone is twisted." Two weeks later, I got operated on and they put in a metal plate. I have it even now, with six screws. I don't have problems with it or with my hand. You just adapt, you know. If a dog doesn't have one leg, he gets around with three legs and he's still the same dog. You can adapt.

You know that when you step in the cage; nobody is going to help you. Just the corner man, if you trust him, but you are really there alone. I've had thirteen matches. My record is not that good, because in the beginning I was just a fighter. I would start training in November and fight in January or February. In my second fight, I dislocated my leg because the guy took a toe hold, but I didn't give up. The referee asked me if I wanted to give up and I said, "No, I don't give up." But I choked the guy out, because I got disgusted and I choked him out.

I don't say I'm tough. I don't know how I am, but when I go there it doesn't matter what happens. I'm going to stay in the game until I'm unconscious. If I'm not conscious, then that's it. Some people ask why I fight—this is the most common question. Some people fight because of the adrenaline. Some people fight because of the fame. I don't know what I'm fighting for. I really don't know. If you ask me to explain in one word why I fight, I really can't tell you. But I like it.

JAMES MEALS was trained in Chinese Kenpo, karate, Brazilian jiu jitsu, boxing, and Muay Thai. He fought in kickboxing and Muay Thai and now fights as a pro MMA fighter and boxer.

I don't even call it fighting—a rush. I could call it a passion, though I don't like to use that word, but it's just something that you can only get from fighting, from MMA, from competition. It's indescribable. See, that's the thing about getting hit in the head! It's an indescribable feeling, yeah, but it's a sport in which you find out after your first fight if you can do it or not. A lot of guys talk about it and they really want to do it, but the first time they get hit, they realize "Holy crap! I'm not a fighter!" Or when you take your first loss, you realize that you are a competitor—I won't even call it a fighter. Some people have it and some people don't. You can get a guy who fights a bunch of bums and he wins 6–0, and then he fights someone with legitimate skills and he loses. Then he's done, because he can't take losing.

I try not to have too much pride, but, you know, the guys who are in tears are the real competitors; they're the guys who really want to win. Everyone calls them the "sissies" of the sport. "Hey, why are you crying on national TV or why are you crying in front of a couple thousand people?" People don't understand it. It's frustration, it's pride, it's just all these emotions hitting you at once! And the only thing you can do is cry because you can't go crazy; you can't try to fight the guy again no matter how much you want to. You can't press the pause button and start over. It's not a video game. It's just an adrenaline rush. It's being angry, mad, sad, everything all at once. And then come the tears.

Then there's the decision-making: are you going to be a fighter or not? First of all, if you don't have pain, you're not training hard enough, or you're not training at the right place. But dealing with it is completely mental. Honestly, I just forget about it and push through it. Pain in practice is nothing compared to when you have pain in the fight. You just have to push through. It's more mental than it is anything else. And the guys who become great are the guys who realize that's what it really is—mental. You have to be mentally tough in order to do this. If you're not, you can forget about it.

I really don't consider a broken nose an injury anymore. It's kind of normal. I've had knee surgery, and when you get your knee worked on, it gets reinjured, and it's twice as hard for it to heal. So knee injuries hurt like crazy. Fractured hands, too. I had an infection in my hand once. I don't know how I got it past the athletic commission or the ring doctor. I used to work for a cement company, and I had a blister on my hand that I pulled off because it was annoying me. I got cement in it and didn't realize that it would get infected. Two weeks later, I was in the middle of a training camp and the back of my hand puffed up. So I pushed it and the front of my hand puffed. And I was like, "Oh shit! This is not good." That was the day before my fight in Massachusetts, a Muay Thai fight. The day before my fight, I was in the emergency room until one in the morning. They poked my hand with a knife to lance it and stuffed a drain inside my hand. The doctor said, "You're going to have to rest, but I told him, "Doctor, I can't. I've got to fight tomorrow night, up in Massachusetts." And he says, "You can't fight," so I said, "Alright, whatever, doc, no problem." But I drove up there that same day. I didn't sleep, I just drove up there, and I fought. Right before a fight, you have to have a physical where they check everything. I covered my hand with a Band-aid, and when the doctor squeezed my hand, I didn't scream. He made me open and close my hands, but I didn't scream and that was it. So I fought with that staph infection in my hand and nobody knew. I lost the decision, couldn't use my hand, really. I went back to the hotel and cut the tape off. The infection in my hand just exploded. When I went back for a checkup in Jersey, the doctor said, "You could have died!" He said, "I know it's just in your hand, but that's a staph infection. You could have died. You were lucky."

That's probably one of the worst things I ever fought through. You get the normal aches and pains, tight back, knees, knots on your chin and feet, hematomas everywhere. It's normal. But like I said, if you're not mentally strong, then you can't fight through it. If you can't fight through it in your head, then you're going to let pain end your career.

ANDY RUGGIERO is a 4th degree black belt in judo. He was the 1993 National Champion, a 1993 World Team Member, and nine-time National Place Winner. Andy has participated in mixed martial arts and has twenty-five years of judo teaching experience.

GOKOR CHIVICHYAN is a 9th degree black belt in judo, 6th degree black belt in Sambo, and 6th degree black belt in jiu jitsu. He moved from Armenia to Los Angeles when he was seventeen years old and trained with Gene LeBell. Gokor has won numerous championships in Europe and America. As a professional, he has competed in more than 400 professional no-holds-barred, judo, and Sambo fights and has never lost. He teaches students and professional fighters at his own school, Hayastan MMA Academy in North Hollywood, California.

CRISTIANO SOUZA came from Brazil to America with a Capoeira team and began training in Brazilian jiu jitsu. He decided to become a mixed martial arts fighter and competes as a welterweight in professional fights.

RANDY BARROSO is a professional mixed martial arts fighter from Venezuela in the lightweight class. He has fought in Venezuela, Holland, and the United States. Randy also owns a martial arts gym in Venezuela where he trains fighters.

MARCOS ("PARRUMPINHA") DA MATTA earned

his 4th-degree black belt in Brazilian jiu jitsu from Carlson Gracie. He competed as a bantam and featherweight in jiu jitsu and became a champion in both weight classes. He won a silver medal in the Mundial and a silver medal in the Pan American Games. Marcos has competed in mixed martial arts fights and is a coach and trainer of professional fighters at American Top Team and also has his own school.

Soccer was my passion and when I started practicing soccer, I got to know Carlson Gracie. We met on the Copacabana Beach, where I used to play football and beach soccer; he was always a fan of the sport. He made jokes or placed bets on the games, and since the first day we met, he was always trying to get me involved in Brazilian jiu jitsu. I never wanted it. Like any Brazilian kid, I wanted to be a soccer player. But he said, "I think you gonna do good, you gonna do good in jiu jitsu. You are very agile and very fast. I think you are going to do very good." But, I never wanted it. So one day I said, "You know what? This old man has been bothering me for six months now, so I'm going to go for maybe one or two weeks and train for a little bit." And then, after a while, I'll say, "Listen. I see, I try, I don't like it. I want to go back to my soccer routine." But jiu jitsu is very addictive. That was the winter of 1987, and now, twenty-four years later, I'm here in the United States teaching and part of one of the biggest MMA teams in the world. I can never forget the huge importance that Carlson Gracie had on my entire life. He was the one who gave me all my belts, and I'm really proud of it. Some people just get there as a blue belt, a purple belt, even a brown belt. They just get one or two belts. I'm really proud that every single belt—even the blue belt—Carlson tied around my waist.

So I started doing tournaments. My first tournament I won in two divisions, my weight and the age division higher. I was pretty lucky that it was the right time with the right people, so I kept competing. I kept winning. Then, maybe one or two years later, I was the tiny kid no more. I used to be small, but now I was a champion.

It's amazing. Once you get some confidence, you walk differently, you act differently. You actually pose yourself differently. So, that changed a lot. Jiu jitsu changed my life for the better, you know. When I was younger, I was very tiny and I used to get picked on a lot in school. So at school things changed a little bit. I never picked a fight. I was never the guy that would go after fights, but then I could say, "You know what? I'm not looking for it, but if those guys come and mess around with me, I'm going to defend myself." That kept happening, you know. It's funny, but there was a guy everybody was afraid of. I was scared of him, too. But after I trained jiu jitsu, I could pretty much do what I knew how to do if this guy came and messed around with me. He was a lot taller, like 5' 10" or 5' 11", but I kicked his ass and the entire school saw it. I went to his back and choked him out. He tapped but I didn't let go, and he went to sleep. There was a lot of anger at that choke, but afterwards I felt a little bad, you know, because knowing how to fight doesn't give me the right to do things like that with people. He didn't have the right to do the things he used to do with me, but now that I know how to fight, I don't think I was right either. Everybody said, "Wow! What a difference!" At that moment, he changed, too, so I think it was a good thing. He completely stopped bullying the other kids, and he respected me a lot. Maybe ten or fifteen years later, he met me in a nightclub, and he was really scared of me, because by then I was already very well known in my city as one of the best jiu jitsu fighters at the time. I used to compete on TV. So that changed a lot. Those guys got terrified when they saw me.

PETER STORM is a black belt in judo and a practitioner of karate, jiu jitsu, and boxing. He founded the Underground Combat League (UCL) in the New York City area and hosts unsanctioned MMA events in all the boroughs of New York. Peter is the promoter, but he also fights on the card. He is employed as a bouncer.

I grew up in the South Bronx, and I used to alternate living there and in Washington Heights, which is also a very tough neighborhood. At a young age, maybe the first grade, I dabbled in the martial arts, but it didn't really grab my attention until the age of ten, when I was at a much higher maturity level. Once I left the gym, my life was chaos. I got my first black belt in July of 1991, two weeks after my fourteenth birthday. About two months after that, I did my first incarceration as a juvenile for assault, and I ended up spending the next two years in juvenile detention. I guess it was a blessing in disguise. My being incarcerated probably saved a lot of people. It was a pretty bad assault, but my conviction was more about my being a juvenile delinquent in family court than about the actual offense. Judge Judy Sheindlin (before she became a TV star) felt that it was necessary to put me away. That and the fact that I told off her husband, who was my original judge, which wasn't the smartest thing. I think that was what actually really sealed my fate.

After I was released at the age of sixteen, I got a job giving out flyers for a club promoter, who saw me in a fight one day outside a club. I beat the shit out of three guys, three other promoters. My boss thought, "That's amazing. You need to start working in the clubs." Here I am, sixteen years old, 160 pounds, still in high school, and he offered me a job as a bouncer. Eventually, I became a full-time bouncer and I worked at some of the toughest clubs in the city. One time we had to throw some Jamaican guys out. They were associated with a well-known gang called the Jamaican Shower Posse, and they came back and shot the club up. There were a couple of us outside. We had to dive because these guys had machine guns. When Jamaicans shoot, they shoot to kill.

With no exaggeration, I have probably been in some 200 fights, as a kid growing up in the streets and as a bouncer. Even to this day, I still get people who will press their luck with me. They don't know that I'm a martial arts master. There are many things I can do to them, but sometimes people find out the hard way. You don't want to go overboard unless you have to, but there are plenty of times when you have to. Just last year, I had a guy who pressed the wrong buttons and we had it out in a staircase. It looked like a murder scene; there was blood everywhere. I got fired for that, but at the end of the day it was okay; he shouldn't have put his hands on me. I justify it based on the way I live my life. If I didn't have the martial arts background, I don't think that I would be in this industry. My martial arts are everything in this business.

I started the Underground Combat League (UCL) in 1999. I had been arrested for a domestic dispute when I caught my girlfriend with another guy. I beat them both up and ended up doing a year in Rikers Island. That year in Rikers Island, I was thinking, like what the fuck do I want to do? I want to do something that nobody else is doing. I remember going to underground fight shows in Canal Street when I was eleven or twelve years old, and I was kind of fascinated by it. I grew up around violence, and when you see violence personified and sensationalized with a spotlight on it, it attracts you. I still see a lot of those fights frame for frame in my mind, and a lot of people's faces and expressions. So when I was sitting in this jail cell in Rikers Island, I was thinking about that. I was fascinated by the Ultimate Fighting Championships, which had come out a couple of years earlier. It was very similar to what we had seen on Canal Street. I had always wanted to do that stuff because I felt I was skilled, but I just didn't have the

PETER STORM'S JUDO CLUB

UCI
UNDERGROUND COMBAT LE

WARRIORS
MMA TEAM

body weight to do it and probably the maturity. When I left Rikers in 2000, I started putting the word out in the martial arts community that I was going to put together a fight club. There was a lot of skepticism. A couple of months after my release, I was staying with a bipolar grandmother under the conditions of my parole. My grandmother had one of those days where she was on the other side of the wall, and she pulled a gun on me. Long story short, I gave her the hip toss from hell. I tell people this, and they're like, "You kicked your grandmother's ass?" Your fuckin' right I did, she pulled a gun on me. I honestly couldn't believe I did this. I was used to doing this to Japanese friends and tough guys, but I just hit a fifty-plus-year-old lady with it. So I ran into my room. I grabbed whatever I could carry, cut off the ankle bracelet, and jumped into a cab. I ended up violating the conditions of my parole.

When I was released in 2001, I was still trying to figure out my way. I was back in the club scene as a bouncer and decided to follow up with this fight club. Finally, in February 2003, I launched my first fight show. It wasn't easy. The most surprising thing about setting up your first fight show is that everybody is "Yeah, yeah, yeah," but when it's time to show up for the fight, everybody's sick or they got lost in traffic. It's kind of a shock, because you want to take people at their word. In the seven years at my club, eighty-five percent of the people who said they were going to show never showed. I think probably ninety, maybe even ninety-five, percent who compete in my league will never do anything with their careers.

It takes something very special to compete in a league like mine, basically because of the rules. We like the old school UFC 1 rules. We don't do biting, eye gouging, fish hooking, or groin shots. But other than that, good luck, gentlemen! Without a doubt, I have the toughest league in the country. I competed in my very first show and won the first fight against a Savate champ. I choked him out. The second fight, I fought a guy that I knew who had fought in cage fights already. I wanted to test my skills. He caught me in an armbar. I didn't tap and my arm snapped. He went, "Are you all right?" I went, "You heard that?" He said, "Yeah." We just got up like nothing and shook hands. The ref asked what happened and we just said "broken."

Normally, what I do is call the guy I want to fight. Or, I call his trainer and say that I was very impressed with his fight and I definitely want to match myself against him. As long as they're comfortable with it, I'm all for it, too. It might sound kind of funny, but there's no animosity or anything. It's just the thrill of competing, especially at this level, because nobody gets paid. I'm the promoter and I get my promoter's salary, but the fighters don't get paid. They're here just for the experience and this is where they will see whether they want to continue or not.

MARCUS "CONAN" SILVEIRA is a pioneer in mixed martial arts. Conan Silveira came to the U.S. already a 7th degree black belt in Brazilian jiu jitsu, under legendary Carlson Gracie. He began his Mixed Martial Arts career in 1993 at Extreme Fighting Battle Cage. At six foot three and 242 pounds, he was the heavyweight champ and during his career obtained four championship belts. He is now a co-owner of American Top Team, a trainer, and a coach.

Anybody who says they don't have fear, they probably are the ones who have more fear than anybody. And the reason why is because you cannot refuse a feeling, or emotion, or excitement. What I believe, in my opinion, for the experience I have for all these years doing this, is that you control your fears. I believe in controlling your emotions; I believe that you have to deal with yourself. That makes you able to get in the stage in the mode that you say, "I'm okay, I'm enjoying that." And it's funny, because that is one of the first things I try to pass to my guys. The guys I train, I tell, you got to feel that, you got to, number one, not refuse that emotion. You do not say "I don't want to feel like that," because you do. But I make that an enjoyment, make that a pleasure. Make that your time, your moment. Bring the positive side of the big pressure, because it doesn't matter that people say, "Oh, I have 200 fights. I don't feel." You do. Every single time it's going to be a different fight, a different time, a different moment. People take examples like Fedor, or George St. Pierre "Oh, it looks like they can look into that face, they don't have that fear." Of course, they do. The difference is how they control that fear. How they deal with that moment. They don't allow the fear to stop them. They're thinking what they want to do in the fight.

I believe so much that the psychological side, as a fighter, that it is something very hard and very difficult to train somebody. You can train with technique. You can make somebody with excellent condition, but mind-wise, it is something that, I got to say, that the majority, the percentage has to be born with you. You got to be born with that. Of course, some guys, they will eventually get there. They want so much, they desire so much, that they will learn how to deal with fear. And it is funny, but you see guys with incredible talent. What happened with the guys that have incredible talent? They train you so hard. You know they are ready, but when it comes to the time, the last five minutes before they are knocking at your door, they say you're next, pretty much, the guys that have all the gold will lose everything. Because, mind-wise, they don't know how to deal with the pressure. I don't know, maybe it has to do with my personality, the way I am. I love the pressure. I'm the opposite way, I love the pressure. I love the moment. I think that we train so hard for three or four months, then you want that fifteen minutes to come. I want—if I could I would make the slow motion so I would enjoy every second. I think the best thing to say is, you know, I just don't believe anybody who says, "I don't have fear." You are forced to do it. You're alive. You have blood, you know, running in your veins. So you got to have the feeling.

RICARDO ALMEIDA is a 3rd degree black belt in Brazilian jiu jitsu, which he teaches at his school in New Jersey. He was a protégé of Carlos Gracie, Jr. and Renzo Gracie. As a mixed martial arts fighter, Ricardo competed in the UFC and PRIDE and was a King of Pancrase middleweight champion. He is now retired from fighting but teaches, coaches at Almeida Brazilian Jiu Jitsu Academy, and works as a judge for New Jersey MMA events.

I was fifteen when I started training jiu jitsu at the Gracie Barra Academy in Brazil, which was very small back then, though it grew into a powerhouse of jiu jitsu, with most of the world champions coming out of there. Renzo Gracie was the most decorated black belt in school, and I grew up trying to emulate him. When I came to the United States, I helped him teach in Philadelphia and accompanied him on trips to Japan, so I started to develop a taste for mixed martial arts

I went, with Renzo's brother Rorion, on a trip to Japan at the end of 2000, when I was twenty-three. He was supposed to fight Kazushi Sakuraba, and we went there two weeks before the fight to train. The second week, a Brazilian guy got hurt, and I was slated to fight Akira Shoji, who, back then, had only lost to heavyweights. He was a pretty tough guy for my first fight; I weighed about 198 pounds, but back then they didn't even have weight divisions, but they would try to match fighters who were more or less the same weight.

Three days before the fight, I started to prepare myself mentally. Even though I had been in the corner, which is very close to the action, it's very different. But I had a great fight; I just was in the zone and my instincts were good. I had never really sparred in boxing before. I knew a little bit how to throw a jab, but I had only really done grappling and had never put on boxing gloves and headgear before. But jiu jitsu had given me good fighting instincts, in terms of relative distances. Renzo gave me advice the whole time. He's an amazing corner man; he really knows what to say and when to say it. And I could hear everything he said, because in Japan the crowd is very quiet. I don't know how I won—it was really beginner's luck—but it was a unanimous decision and I really dominated the fight.

A couple of years later, Renzo and his two brothers were going against three Japanese in the Challenge Bushido, but Renzo got hurt and couldn't fight, so he asked me to take his place. This was by far my biggest honor. It was great, but it was a lot of pressure and I don't think I would want to do it again. I felt what it was like to be a Gracie for a day, and it was a lot of weight on my shoulders, but we won.

A lot of people fight because it's the only thing they know how to do, or they fight for the money because they've gotta make a living. Other people fight because of their ego, so if you're getting in there with a big ego, more likely than not you're gonna leave without it, because everyone loses at one time or another, especially in mixed martial arts. There are not a lot of undefeated fighters who have been fighting for more than three or four years. Everyone loses. So if you're in there with a big ego, you're gonna have a hard time. It's different if you're in there for a good reason. For me, it was always about representing my school, representing jiu jitsu. I will do my best not to tarnish the legacy of eighty years of victories in jiu jitsu and just set a good example for the guys who will come after me.

I also love that challenge, being at the edge of the cliff and having to decide whether I'm going to go for it or not. For me, that challenge has been my motivator all throughout my competitive career. You want to win, you want to do well, you want to have a successful career, although I knew early on that I wasn't going to make a career out of fighting.

Fear is a good thing; or at least it's not a bad thing and it keeps you honest. It keeps you on your toes and makes you move quickly, probably more quickly than you would move if you were too relaxed. There is no courage if there isn't fear. And if there's no fear, it's just craziness. It's just someone being angry trying to hurt the other guy. I embrace fear as being part of the fight.

Sometimes it gets away from me and then it comes back, and I get real nervous and get punched. Fear just makes things calm down. It's really a part of fighting. I don't think a lot of fighters are afraid of being hurt. I don't think that anybody fears they will get a black eye. I think what they really fear is public failure. You know, like you're not living up to what you are supposed to do. Sometimes you blank and sometimes you move just slow enough to allow the other guy to be faster. It's not a race. It's not about being fast, and the other guy gets there before you. It's a contest to see who is going to hit who first, and if your hand doesn't get there and his does, that's it. Fight over.

VINCENT MARCHETTI

Chuck Wepner says that his good friend Marchetti is one of the toughest guys he knows. Coming from Chuck, that's saying a lot. Marchetti, who is now over seventy, has a 10th-degree karate black belt, a 7th-degree jujitsu black belt, and a 3rd-degree judo black belt. Although he is now primarily a martial arts instructor, he began his career as an amateur boxer and underground fighter. He was introduced to the trade by his uncle, Joe Turko, a boxer.

Back in the 1950s and '60s, my mother and father went back and forth to Texas, and I used to live with my Uncle Joe, who was known as "Turk." He taught me to box. I used to work in his basement punching a speed bag, punching a heavy bag. He had the old ways of training: he would tie your feet together so you couldn't go with a wide span. He put pennies in my hands, and if a penny fell while I was banging on the bags, he would slap me with a stick because that meant my hand was open or loose. He used to do all these old tricks, like slapping me across the face constantly so I wouldn't be afraid to get hit. I learned at the Village Boys Club and the Paul Revere Club, both in Jersey City. He always made me spar against bigger kids, and most of them downtown in Jersey City were black. He owned a club downtown in Jersey City called the Four Aces, and he was All-Service Heavyweight Champ when he was in the Navy. As I grew up, I looked up to him, and fighting was my way after that. I'm not big, but I was always considered very fast and a good quick thinker. I learned how to win quickly.

I fought in factories for money in Secaucus, where the gangsters would put the fights on in either abandoned factories or factories that closed on the weekend. You'd fistfight and there was no referee. All these limos and yuppies from New York would come and pay to watch and bet on you. I don't know how popular it was, but I know it drew a lot of New York City people. I used to see all those cars from New York, all different kinds of fancy cars. And people paid probably twenty bucks to get in, one time twenty-five dollars.

Secaucus back then was all pig farms and old beat-up factories, like metalwork factories or slaughterhouses, where they would have the fights in the 1950s. And it was popular. I didn't know about it until somebody turned me on to it: "You want to go. We need a fighter?" I said okay. I didn't know it was going to be so brutal, but at the time, my ego wouldn't let me say no. I needed the money bad.

I did seven matches. There was one phone on the floor where I lived, and they would call and tell me they were gonna call on a Thursday night for a Saturday night fight. "We'll tell you where it is and you're gonna tell us you're gonna fight." That's all they wanted to hear, you know? "If you refuse us once, we may never come back to you." So I did it seven times and sometimes it would be three weeks or a month between fights. A lot of them were just street fighters, bar fighters, and things like that. They just wanted the money. You would get your knees dislocated and break your toes, break your fingers. I always carried different-sized Popsicle sticks to use as splints for my toes so I could tape them together. I carried needle-nose pliers that were made of hard rubber so that I could put my own nose septum back in place and pack my nose so I could fight again that same night. I would always carry my own wraps for my ribs and my own Ace bandages.

Nobody wore gloves, and nobody wore shoes. You could wear sneakers if you wanted to, back then, but I didn't wear any, and most of the other guys didn't wear them either. We didn't have groin cups then; guys would make their own, because people would try to knee or kick you in the groin. You would do everything you could to cheat in different ways. Some guys would even do things like putting something in their mouth to cut you, but their reputation would get known, so you'd know exactly how to handle them. There was always a doctor who would stop the fight if there was either too much blood or a broken bone. He would make sure if you were knocked out. That's the only way the fight would end.

I won my share of those fights. I made more money in one night than my father would make in a month. The weight divisions were broken down into just light and heavy. If you won your three fights, you made your money, a hundred bucks a shot.

I wasn't allowed to refuse. One time they said, "You wanna get paid?" And I said, "You promised to pay me." And they came back with, "Yeah, we're gonna pay you, but you're gonna fight the heavyweight. You won all the fights and people like you, and you're popular, and you won 'em pretty fast. You're gonna fight the heavyweight." I didn't think that was fair, but I really didn't have a choice. I figured I'd just let him knock me out, or fake it if I had to. Then the fight would end, although the guy would pound on you. I know it because I had seen him fight. So I went out there and he saw my ribs were taped from previous fights. They told me not to tape them because he would recognize and crush me 'cause he was big, 267 pounds, maybe about six-three. And so he did. He picked me up and he started crushing me. I put my thumbs in his eyes, bit his nose, and put a choke on him. He fell down and I kept choking him and then they pulled me off. And I won the fight. I became popular.

I got a twenty-dollar tip coming off that fight. And twenty dollars back then was what people made in a week. All along, they had been giving me a bunch of singles, maybe a five dollar bill, but this guy gave me a twenty. Later on, I was walking from Secaucus to get the bus, which is a seven- or eight-mile walk, and a 1958 Corvette pulled up next to me with New York plates. The driver offered me a ride, which I refused 'cause I thought he was gay. I said, "I don't want to take the ride," but he told me, "I saw you fight. I gave you twenty. Remember me?" So I got in the car, and he drove me up to Journal Square.

I spent all the money I made that night for an older Corvette. I was living then in a furnished, dollar-a-day room next to the bar in Union City, but I bought a Corvette and I was the richest kid, poorest kid, all at the same time. And since then I have never been without a Corvette. At one time, I had the largest antique Corvette dealership on the East Coast in Pompano, Florida. But when I bought that '56 Corvette, I was paying a dollar a day for my bed and my sink, and I shared a bathroom with ten other people, and yet I had a Corvette. I felt like the richest kid alive.

ALFIE BUCK is a former street fighter who trained in judo, jiu jitsu, and boxing. He was an early participant in mixed martial arts, beginning in 1996 with illegal events. He now fights in mixed martial events and teaches MMA.

I was definitely the minority in my neighborhood, so it was do or die. I came up through all the rough schools because my parents were poor and we moved into some bad areas. So, I was involved in a lot of street fights, but I was good at fighting, which has a lot to do with what I do now. I definitely surprised a lot of bigger people when I worked as a bouncer, when my weight was about 180 pounds. You get big, burly bikers who are used to intimidating people and smacking them around. So, when you've got to handle business, you actually scoop one of them up and walk him out of the bar. My fellow bouncers were always laughing and joking about that, about the look on the guy's face when he got scooped up by me.

I had started out boxing because I wanted to be some kind of athlete. I got locked into a contract with some people, and it was a nightmare. I actually did only one pro fight, but then I started watching the UFC on TV. I was a good boxer and a good puncher, and with my background in judo I figured it would be an easy transition. I answered an ad in *Black Belt* magazine and ended up on the show. I sent them a demo tape and ended up fighting in a few tournaments, and it just kept going from there.

The first time I fought mixed martial arts was in 1996, when it was illegal everywhere, so every time I fought, I had to go out of state, to Iowa, Michigan, or Virginia. I fought Pat Miletich back in 1998. He was number one in the world when I fought him, and he was the UFC champ. He was also an Extreme Fighting champion, some kind of kick boxer, and a Muay Thai boxing champion when I fought him. Once I could lay the leather on him, he went in for and got the take-down and ended up tapping me out. I didn't get paid anything for that fight, although that night I won three grand in the casino on the riverboat, so I ended up making out pretty good on that one.

I would love to be ten years younger. Now MMA is getting to the general public. It's not just the hard core fans that read *Black Belt* or *Grapplers* magazines. Now, everyday people know about it and it's already on regular TV. It's starting to get a big following; even movie stars are coming to events. I've got a few years left, maybe ten, at least five. There's something about wanting people to enjoy themselves. You feel like a rock star when you go out there. There's nothing like it, you know. Afterwards, if you put on a bad performance, nobody wants to talk to you. But if you put on a good performance, even if you lose, people still love you. So if you put your heart out there, they're going to remember you.

ROB GUARINO is a mixed martial arts fighter. He also trains and coaches MMA fighters.

JOSE RODRIQUEZ boxed while he was in the U.S. Marine Corps. When he left the service, he began training as a mixed martial art fighter. When he left the service, he became a professional MMA fighter.

CHUTIPHAT ("CHA") RUNGSAWANG was a champion in three weight classes as a pro Muay Thai fighter in Thailand. He has trained fighters in Thailand, the Philippines, and the United States.

MIKE TATTOO is a judo back belt who competed in many matches. He worked as a bouncer and was also an arm-wrestling champion. He was a cast member of the HBO series *Oz*.

DOUG ANDERSON enlisted in the U.S. Army in 2002 and served in Iraq, where his unit was involved in numerous battles for which he received several decorations. He has been a boxer and has a blue belt in Brazilian jiu jitsu. After returning from Iraq, he fought in MMA events and was a co-star on the Discovery Channel show *Fight Quest*. On the show, he traveled around the world to study with the masters of various martial arts for five days, after which he had to fight experts in each art.

By the time I was ten, I had fought at least a hundred fights, usually one a week. I mellowed out a lot when I got to be a teenager, when we moved to a nicer area. It wasn't as rough, so I didn't fight a whole lot, but it was kind of like in me already. I was used to fighting. It was something that I loved to do. Then I got a couple of concussions and doctors told me that I shouldn't fight anymore. So I stopped for a long time. And then, when I joined the Army, it kind of got me into it again, because you train combatives in the Army and you get a little bit of fighting in. And that stuff just whetted my appetite.

When I was in Iraq, I realized how much I dug the adrenaline rush of danger. I guess I always knew that, but I really knew it for sure after spending time in Iraq. We would go on patrols every day and I'd say, "Man, I hope somebody shoots at us today." I remember the first time bombs went off around us. We were sitting in our trailers, just hanging out and talking, and you hear BOOOOOM! We look outside and we can see the smoke plume, maybe fifty yards from our trailer. And then BOOM, BOOM, BOOM! Mortars are dropping all around us, rockets. It was cool. Everybody reacted differently. Some people were real serious, some were freaking out. One kid I remember was just spinning around in circles. But I was just, like, "Yeah! Let's go! Let's do it!" The adrenaline, you know. It feeds me. There was never any fear. I've never really been afraid of death. I fear failure. I don't want to mess up. I don't want to let people down. But death doesn't scare me.

For me, especially when I first got back from Iraq, fighting was therapy. It was a way to exorcise the demons. Somebody who allowed me to punch them was doing me a huge favor. And when somebody punched me, I felt like the more pain that I received, the more I would be redeemed, the more forgiveness I would get, like a penance.

On the *Fight Quest* show, Krav Maga in Israel probably was the hardest one that we did, for multiple reasons. The worst-case scenario was being in a fight with no rules, and when they say no rules, they mean absolutely no rules. In the event, I had my throat bitten three or four times, I had people gouging my eyes. My brand new cup was shattered by the end of the week from people stomping on my balls. The only protective gear you wore was your cup, so no padding. You're going bare knuckle and knees and elbows; that's pretty nuts. And then on top of those two negative factors, you're fighting multiple opponents, four or five guys at once with no pads and no rules. It was mayhem, complete insanity. I would wake up every day to train Krav Maga and worry if I was going to make it through the day. Every time I was about to fight there, I would say a little prayer.

I read a quote from a famous Japanese samurai who said that the way of the warrior is death, so whenever there is a choice between life and death, the warrior must choose death. So I would say a prayer and repeat that quote to myself and look at my opponents and be like, "I choose death." I accepted death if that's what was going to happen, because I honestly felt like there was a chance I was going to die. My first night there, I had a guy stomping on my brainstem, like for at least forty seconds straight. I'm the type of person who can't quit. I can't back down. I can't give up. Unless you knock me unconscious, I'm going to keep going. I don't care if you're making me retarded or whatever, I'm not going to give up and say, "Hey this isn't fair." So yeah, there was a lot of fear because sometimes I didn't know that I was going to make it.

The other crazy one was Kyokushin karate. I fought nine guys in a row, all a little bit bigger than me; one guy was 205 to 210 pounds, the Japanese national champion. These dudes were great people, but nasty, nasty fighters. On the show, I am only seen sparring with three guys in a row, but it was really nine guys and I got knocked out at least five times. I would fight a dude for a minute, and then they would send in a new guy who was fresh. Kyokushin is like balls to the wall action the whole time, so by six minutes or so, I was dead tired and these guys were still fresh. So I would get knocked out and scramble back to my feet as soon as I woke up. Most of them were like flash knockouts, so I would just drop, have a dream real quick, pop up, and not even know where I was. I just knew there was a guy in front of me, so I started swinging. My instructor would be beating me in the back with a bat, not a baseball bat but a wooden staff, screaming at me to keep fighting. That was tough.

I took a Tae Kwon Do class when I was in third grade, the closest I ever got to formal martial arts. I never had a ton of interest in it, but it appeals to me a little bit more now. Some of it is really cool stuff, really beautiful. You know, if you want to be a good fighter, mixed martial arts is the way to go. There's a lot of beauty and spiritually in the art aspect of martial arts, and I like that a lot.

There's definitely a common mentality amongst fighters. I've really pondered it and tried to figure out what it is that causes us this weird bond between fighters. There is definitely a personality archetype that is attracted to this type of thing. I'd say that the two groups I've made the best friends with in my entire life have been in the Army and in fighting gyms. I guess the source for that is the bond that comes through mutual hardship.

GLEISON TIBAU is a black belt in Brazilian jiu jitsu who fought in forty-six vale tudo matches in his native Brazil. When he came to the United States, he was signed up by the Ultimate Fighting Championship, where he competes in MMA events in the lightweight division.

I started doing martial arts when I was thirteen years old after watching some Jean-Claude Van Damme movies. I come from a small town in Brazil, and the martial arts school was thirty miles away from my house. I started training hard, and I fought my first fight in martial arts when I was fifteen. After this, I never stopped and kept training hard. Then I moved to Rio de Janeiro to train in a bigger school, and I did a lot of fights in Rio. Eventually, I moved to the United States and joined the American Top Team. In my third month there, I signed a contract for the Ultimate Fighting Championship. That was the right time in the right spot. I was lucky to get in because they needed fighters in the 170 pound division.

In Brazil, I fought vale tudo, or freestyle. The only difference was the rules. We fought with bare hands, there were no gloves; there was a boxing ring, not a cage. I fought a lot for free just to get the experience,

forty-six fights. When I started, ten years ago, there were no weight divisions. Some of the people that I fought were 190 or 200 pounds, even though I weighed 170. A couple of the fights were in private backyards to make money, because I did some fights free and had to make some money.

There were all types of people in vale tudo, and I fought against guys who were older and bigger. Some shows were two rounds of fifteen minutes each, and some were one round of thirty minutes. Back in the day at these small shows, the fighter had more than one fight. One night I fought twice in the same night to make it to the final match, and one of them was a long fight. My opponent in the final match also fought two fights before we met. He was one of the biggest names, Charles Andre, in his state, but I won, and the promoter gave me a motorcycle. That was the first time I made some money in a big fight, and it was a big win.

RICARDO LIBORIO is a 7th degree black belt in Brazilian jiu jitsu who won the Brazilian National Championship and then the World Championship at Mundial. He has a degree in business administration and completed one year of law school.

My father was a bank manager, and I worked in a bank from the time I was thirteen years old. But I knew I would never be happy working in a bank. I was promoted and became a manager for big accounts, like Xerox and some hospitals. I was doing loans and payrolls, but I just hated it. I knew it wasn't right for me, and I knew I could not do anything extraordinary there. So, in 1995, Carlson Gracie told me that I had to get back to training. "There's the National Championship in '95. You've got to compete. We are going to need somebody there." So I competed and I won the Brazilian National Championship, which meant I was automatically entered in the World Championships. I talked to the superintendent of the bank and got a sponsorship to compete in the World Championship.

From then on, my life really changed. I competed in the World Championship and I won. That brought a lot of recognition and publicity, which was a cheap form of marketing for the bank. I was awarded the most technical black belt and it got a lot of attention because I was a bank manager and still found the time to train. At that time, the bank wanted to develop credit cards for teenagers, so I prepared a project and proposed to the bank superintendent that I go to schools and make the teenagers aware of the credit card by talking to them and doing demonstrations. So we created this huge data base for teenagers who went to the good schools in Rio de Janeiro, and it was a great success for the bank. I worked outside the bank for two years, doing the school visits and training. However, the presidency in Brazil changed and the bank hierarchy also changed, and they called me back. But I already knew I couldn't go back to the bank, so I left. I partnered with Murilo Bustamante, Mario Sperry, and Luis Roberto "Bebeo" Duarte, and we created the Brazilian Top Team.

While I was coaching Minotauro (Rodrigo Noguiera) for his fight with Mark Coleman, I was invited to go to Japan with him. But then I met Dan Lambert when I went out to Las Vegas to see Murilo Bustamante fight Chuck Lidell, and Dan said, "Instead of going to Japan, why don't you stay here in the U.S?" So a couple months later, I sold my part of the Brazilian Top Team and partnered with the Silveira brothers to found ATT (American Top Team). It was a pretty bold move at the time, but I quickly realized that we had something really big here. Dan was our financial investor and he played a big role in my life. It was the perfect time for a move, because I was single then and didn't have kids. Now we are considered one of the best MMA teams in the world, one of the best grappling teams. The great thing about ATT is that it isn't about me; all the coaches are responsible for the success of the team, and the losses too. We all play together and everybody has a part.

You can lose, but that doesn't mean that you're a loser. How many really big champions have lost and come back? To come back is the true beauty of everything. You can be a champion and be defeated and come back. What people can't understand is that it is okay for you to lose, but it is not okay for you to quit. You've got to go back there and try to perform better; you've still got to have the flame to be a winner, to be a champion. And keep going, going, going. You've got to be humble enough even when you are at the top to remember when you didn't know anything. Now I know something and I'm very good at it, but somebody can still come along and win, maybe because you're sick, or sad, or because you have a personal problem. It's part of the process to becoming a winner. Overcome and develop, that's the name of the game.

All the high-level guys that I have worked with, I have seen those guys in tears, At the highest level, when you see a guy who is training, training, and ready to fight and gets his butt kicked for some reason, he'll leave the gym crying or sad because he thinks he failed that day. There is always a bad day of training, and there always will be. I've seen all the professional fighters get very upset, but there is always a tomorrow. You can't get caught up in the turmoil of depression. You've just got to do the right thing, follow the schedule.

Most people can hide their emotions because they're not very exposed. But fighters expose themselves in competition more than regular people, not just to getting hurt but to the humiliation of defeat. That's what really hurts. It's different from a lot of other jobs. Before a fight, you know you want to do the best you can, and it's just impossible not to be nervous. But at the time of the fight, things change. Your mindset, your reflexes, your muscle memory, your technique—all of it is almost like being on autopilot. I've known fighters who can't remember their fights right afterward. In the locker room they ask about the fight, because they don't remember anything—not because they got knocked out, but because they were so emotionally involved that they couldn't remember.

The most exciting moment in my career was winning the World Championship, because I had been defeated in '93 by my rival at the time. But then I beat him in '96. He enrolled in the super heavyweight division, and I went after him. I used to be middleweight, but I enrolled myself in super heavyweight so I could fight him, and I beat him. That was a good feeling. But overall I don't take my accomplishments as a professional fighter as the most satisfying thing. I really get the most satisfaction when our guys win, not just to see them winning, but also to be able to help them. It is part of my nature. I like to help people, and I was always like that. You can't always help everybody, but I try. I have a good feeling about it, maybe for selfish reasons, because it makes me feel good. I like what I do, especially when I'm teaching.

As a coach, you can see the opponent's weaknesses and come up with strategies much more easily than your fighter can. It is easier seeing it from the outside. It is easy to see it, but hard to do it. When you have a good connection with your fighter, he can trust what you see and follow you. Corners can win fights.

During the pressure of a fight, few fighters can work completely without pressure. There are many variables in the game that really count, and few people can stay so relaxed that they can function 100 percent. A lot of success has to do with dedication. You can be very talented, but if you are not up to the training, if you are not dedicated, if you do not follow the schedule, if you don't punch the clock every day, you could become a champion, but you will not be a legend. You've got to put the schedule in, you've got to work hard. Hard work and talent, that's it. I'll take a very hard-working kid with some talent any day over a very talented guy who doesn't want to work.

American Top Team is more than just a team, it's a group of professional fighters in training. It really is a family. That's one of the most important things, you know, why we're here for the long run. I'm here for the long run. I really like what I do. It's like any job: it's not perfect, you deal with all the problems in the world, and every day, especially in MMA training, people have different personalities, different needs, different egos. But the community goes beyond any personal interest in making as much money as I can put in my pocket. I think that my partners and I are here to help, to help the community, to help the family, to share.

I really like my people, and I really like my guys, you know. I really care about them, not just their results as professional fighters, because not everybody is going to make it as a professional fighter. But you give them opportunities in the business, give them a chance to do what they love to do, and you can make a living out of that. It is about happiness, you know. That's very important.

GESIAS "JZ" CAVALCANTE began training in judo in Brazil when he was four years old. He is a black belt in Lute Livre and a brown belt in Brazilian jiu jitsu. He is a mixed martial arts fighter who won the 2006 and 2007 K-1 Heros middleweight championships. He was also a Shooto middleweight champion and has fought in Strikeforce.

JAMES MCLAUGHLIN was trained in karate, jiu jitsu, and judo, and is a former amateur Golden Gloves champion and professional boxer. These skills helped him against attackers in his career as a police officer. He became a detective and served as a liaison with gangs in the South Bronx. He now coaches and trains young boxers.

SCOTTY BRONX has been a bouncer and has worked in private security his entire adult working life. He has trained in various martial arts and boxing.

When I was in junior high school, I was always getting picked on by the school bullies because I had curly hair and glasses and was considered a nerd. But my last year in junior high school, I wound up beating up both school bullies at the same time, and from then on I just put myself into a lot. I started body building when I was fourteen years old, lifting weights and punching with dumbbells to get faster hands. When I grew up, I started hanging out in night clubs, but that life ended when I turned eighteen and started working. Then I started doing private security and private parties, and I got into bouncing.

I was very wild when I was young. One of my managers said, "You could start a fight in a desert by yourself, because that's how wild you are." But I had to prove something, and I had a lot to prove. And, yeah, maybe I caused more than what I should have caused, but you had to get your name out there. I treat people the way I want to be treated, you know, with a lot of respect, and I expect it in return. I don't want to be disrespected. I don't like that overbearing attitude where you're making yourself look good in front of a crowd, but when we are alone, that's a different ballgame. I'm gonna have a problem. I'm gonna get upset, you know.

There was always a trick with the bigger guys. I'm six-one, two-forty pounds, and say I run into a guy who's six-five. You pull him to the side. He's screaming and yelling. So I say to him, "If you want to do this, we can do this, but you gotta remember: you have more to lose than I do. You're a big guy and you beat up a little guy. But if I win, the little guy beat up the big guy. That's all they're gonna remember."

I can read somebody by looking in their eyes, what they're gonna do. You can tell some guys by their body language, if they're shaking, if they're nervous. But some guys you come across and you don't know where it's coming from. That's why I've always carried a mouthpiece. I always put it in the minute I know something is gonna happen. People hesitate because they think, "Why's he's putting a mouthpiece in?" Well, if we're gonna do battle, we're gonna do battle. I don't wanna lose my teeth. So it really deters a lot. A lot of the kids who come into the club aren't trained; some of 'em are. If you're in a multiple fight—say maybe me and three bouncers against eight guys—most of the time, the first guy gets knocked out and the rest of them usually back off. They don't want to get hit. They didn't expect it to go that far.

A lot of people think that bouncers stand there and break up fights and that's it. There's a lot more to it because you gotta go home at night, and some of these crazy kids will come after you. I don't want that problem. I'm always the one they say, "He's a nice guy, just don't fuck with him." And that's the way I always liked it.

PAUL VIZZIO,

PAUL VIZZIO, an underground fighter in the late 1960s and early 1970s, compiled a 55–0 record in matches organized by Asian gamblers. He began to master other disciplines and successfully made the transition from the anything-goes matches of the underground to the rules, referees, and structure of kickboxing. He kickboxed for twenty-three years, amassing a 47–1 record, and for a time was the reigning world champion. Currently, he is a trainer of Kung fu and kickboxing at his school in New Jersey.

We started in the streets, learning how to use different parts of the street, and I became a tough man. Then I became a boxer. I was on the Boys Club Boxing Team from the 1950s to, I guess, the '60s. Then I saw some Chinese guys breaking bricks, and I liked that. That could help me because I was a little guy. So I followed those guys to Chinatown and waited outside the building they went into. I would get some money, a quarter, and buy coffee and offer it to one of them. He refused a couple of times; then he took it a couple of times. Then he opened the door for me.

I lived in Chinatown and they paid for everything. I was a young kid. Matches were set up by different people. You could have one, two, three fights a day. They used to tell me to fight this guy; I didn't know what it was, just fight this guy. There was no referee, only to start the fight but no one to break nothing up. They all backed off because it's bloody. There were no rounds. They say go, and you go. You could bang their head against the wall, against the floor, pipes. Somebody could throw in something for the guy and the guy could use that. If the guy gets up, you got to keep going. That was it. They were billed as death matches. It was only for the Orientals. It was a group of them, maybe fifty or a hundred. These were wealthy people. What happened was they started making a lot of money on it, because they were betting restaurants and stuff like that. And there were a lot of bets going on. I had to get away from Chinatown so I could try to make a living for myself. I wanted to get married but I had no girlfriend. There were no girls, you know. I didn't have that life.

In my late teens, early twenties is when the martial arts thing started going. What I'd been practicing on the bag, what I'd been doing in the air, let me try this. There's fourteen movements. I did that for eleven-and-a-half months. I practiced them over and over and over, those fourteen moves. I had to develop a fighting skill that looked like a martial art. A kick and a punch.

In the early 1970s, I joined PKA, with boxing gloves and foot protectors, kick above the belt and all that. I didn't know about kick above the belt. I didn't know about rounds. I just was this tough guy. I didn't know about endurance and getting tired. I never experienced rules and regulations and referees. The skills and the techniques came later in the PKA, with the professionals teaching how to get endurance and how to hit with the gloves and the kicks. You have to ask for the help. You say, "What am I doing bad? How come that it looks bad?" It becomes technique. Speed is a big factor. If you're there first, you usually have the better chance to win.

Now they got the rules going on and a lot of weight divisions and a lot of fines, and they kind of know when somebody's hurt and they're taken care of. It might be safer than boxing itself right now. And they're in tremendous shape. They're athletes. These guys are not fat slobs, dirty-looking people. It's gotten better.

The people who know me, they're not around. I wish I could go on the Internet and find out some of those funny names that we used to have and see if they're still around, and say, "Come on, come down and see me. I'll go see you." The guys I grew up living with in the projects, from what I heard, the guys are dead or shot or junkies or in jail. I'm one of the lucky ones. Yeah, real lucky.

ROB KAMAN

ROB KAMAN is a Dutch former nine-time world kickboxer and Muay Thai champion fighter who fought at both middleweight and light heavyweight. He is considered by many fight experts to be one of the best kickboxers ever. In 1992, when Rob won the ISKA title by TKO, he was both the Muay Thai world champion and the WKA world champion. He fought throughout Asia and Europe and had 112 fights with 98 wins and 78 knockouts. Currently Rob trains fighters and gives seminars.

When I visited Rob, I found that he has become quite spiritual now and spends his time meditating and reading. I asked if he would have pursued fighting if he were as spiritual then as he is now, because of the violence associated with it. He replied that he would still have fought and would have been even better than he was, because he would have been more focused. He does not consider his fighting a violent sport. He considers it competition.

– J.W

FREDDIE ROACH started boxing when he was six years old. As an amateur, he won the New England AAU Tournament five times and the Golden Gloves once. As a professional boxer, he fought fifty-four times, including bouts with Bobby Chacon and Hector Camacho for the lightweight championship. Freddie owns Wild Card Gym in Los Angeles, where he trains professional boxers and MMA fighters. He is Manny Pacquiao's trainer and has also trained Mike Tyson and Oscar DeLa Hoya, along with many other champions.

HECTOR LOMBARD is a Cuban-Australian mixed martial artist and former Olympic judo competitor. He is a 4th degree judo black belt and won a gold medal at the Australian Open; he also has a black belt in Brazilian jiu jitsu. He left Bellator as an undefeated middleweight champ to fight in the UFC.

DAVE NIELSEN is a Muay Thai fighter, trainer, and a co-owner of American Boxing in San Diego, California. He was accepted to UCLA Law School but realized that he would rather have a career as a Muay Thai fighter. Dave is the current IKF World Muay Thai Champion.

RALPH PASSERO

RALPH PASSERO enrolled in a karate school after completing a tour of Vietnam in the U.S. Army's First Brigade Airborne. He became a 9th degree Dan and Grandmaster in Issin Ryu karate. Ralph has fought in full-contact karate and kickboxing matches and is a former heavyweight full-contact karate champion. He has been a karate instructor since 1970 and owns a karate school in Bayonne, New Jersey.

I had a match with Chuck Wepner in September of 1993. Now that was a match. In order for Chuck and me to fight each other, he had to get relicensed and I had to get licensed. Chuck was over the age and I had just turned fifty. We always do benefits for different organizations, so I was approached by this group, ARC, the Association for Retarded Citizens. They're trying to raise money for these kids. So we were going to run our normal, regular karate tournament, which we run once a year. I said, "Chuck. What do you say? You and I, we get this on. We'll do this for nothing. All the money, all the proceeds, everything, we're going to give to this ARC."

I went from 295 pounds to 250 for the fight. We fought at the Bayonne High School. We started fighting, and at the time I was wearing a hairpiece. Putting this tournament together, I was there from six in the morning until the night when we fought, and I was probably due to get my hair redone, fixed, tightened, reglued, whatever the hell it was, the works. So the match starts and we start fighting and all of a sudden we clash. Chuck grabs hold of me, flips me up in the air, body slams me, throws me to the floor. My head hits first, my hairpiece goes flying. I get up, pick up the hairpiece, and throw it on the announcer's desk (this is on video by the way), and the announcer goes, "This is road kill from the ring." The whole fight stops. Chuck is like, "I'm sorry, Ralph. Jesus Christ!" And I say, "What are you going to do?" It ain't no big thing to me. I didn't care.

So the round continues. I'm keeping my distance because I'm not letting him punch with that good strong left hand. So I throw the kick and he quicksteps in and goes BOOM! I thought I was going out. That's how hard he hit me. So we went back and forth. He's banging me. I'm banging him. I'm kicking him with kicks that I kicked through a sixteen-foot square block of ice. And every time I kicked, it hit Chuck, who went, "Well, that's a good kick, Ralph. That's a good kick." And I'm like, "you mother-fucking ... " And I come in, trying to get closer, trying to connect, and I'm hitting him and hitting him. But it's just not happening, right?

So this goes on and on and on. Finally, at the end of the last round, Chuck is trying to take me out. I'm bleeding. He's not bleeding. The only fight he ever had that he was not bleeding. While the fight is going on, he says, "Just go ahead," and I jump in with a side kick, BOOM! Caught him! And I bent him over. I'm like, "Aw, fuck!" And he gets up. "You fucking hurt me," he said. I said, "I hurt you? I'm half unconscious here, what are you kidding? I only want to finish the round."

They announce that it was a draw. And that was it. When you fight somebody you don't know, you don't care. But when you got a friendship that's like a family-style love, it's kind of hard. Both guys want to win, but you don't want to hurt each other. You want it, you still want to be you here. I couldn't see losing my friendship for thirty years with him and blowing it going out like a maniac. Maybe I should have, because that was what he was doing!

After the fight, we were in a bar laughing. We're pissing in our pants having drinks at Gaetano's, a club that I bounced at. He said, "I'm sore." I said, "You're sore? I got a concussion here, Chuck." I've had concussions, so I know when things ain't right. You feel pressure inside your head. I could imagine how Ali felt. I mean, BANG! BANG! BANG! continuously getting hit here.

GERRY COONEY is a former top-ten heavyweight professional boxer with a 28–3 record, 24 knockouts. He is known for having one of the most powerful left hooks in boxing history.

I was always a puncher.

When I was sixteen, I saw my brother in a street fight and I saw him knock the guy out with a right hand to the head and a left hook to the body, and it was devastating. The guy was out cold on the chin, but he had all of the wind knocked out of him and couldn't breathe. So that's how I became a body puncher. When I was sixteen, I won the state middleweight championship in New York. I was six foot four inches, 160 pounds back then, and I had seven fights and five knockouts to get to the championship. In all, I had fifty-seven amateur fights as a middleweight and lost three, but I had a quite a lot of knock-outs. At a young age, I became a converted southpaw; I'm a leftie, but I fought rightie, so most of the power is in my left hand, and when I jab somebody, it's like I hit him with a regular right hand.

All world-class athletes learn split-second timing to make the connection where you want to connect with devastating power. Those moments are when you can create the punch, set it up without the other person knowing it. It's a magical moment where you can create the shot and it works. It's like a golfer hitting the perfect drive.

Unfortunately, I didn't get the experience I needed. Don King owned almost everybody, so I wasn't able to fight all of his guys, and I fought only once a year. I knocked out Ken Norton in fifty-four seconds, but then I didn't fight for thirteen months. And then I fought Larry Holmes, one of the top fighters in history, and lost. They blamed me for it at the time, but realistically between the promoter, Don King, and my manager, they didn't want to miss out on that big payday, so they kept me shielded from other matches. What I really needed was two or three more fights to have the experience, so I could better handle it. Holmes said that if I had waited another year, I would have beat him.

When I got married and my children were born—those are all great moments in my life. Being a fighter, being number one in the world was a great experience. All of the people I touched and was touched by were great, but that passed. All athletes have to turn the page. The biggest thing they miss is the roar of the crowd, but that day comes, and you have to get on with your life, accept it and move on, but it's all good.

I still train today at fifty-six. I still can slow down the round anytime I want with a little body shot, or hit the guy with a shot to hurt him, in order to slow down the pace of the fight. The thing about punching power is that you never lose it. You just lose some split-second timing, but as long as you're in the gym, you hold onto that as well.

I think everybody can identify with the fight of life. I had to struggle growing up in my background, and people relate to that. I remember the first time someone told me, "Listen, when you knock this guy out tonight, I want you to reach out and touch that crowd, touch those people." And I thought he was crazy, but when I knocked the guy out, I could reach out and touch all of those fans who were cheering for me.

I do a lot of charity work, so I'm around a lot of different people. It's a way for you to relive your life over and over again, and it brings you back to the moment. It's a great moment.

 GYMS

The following list includes gyms that are owned by some of the fighters featured in this book. They are arranged by state with their web sites.

California
American Boxing
www.americanboxing.net

Hayastan MMA Academy
www.Gokor. com and www.genelebell.com

Florida
American Top Team
www.americantopteam.com

New Jersey
Almeida Brazilian Jiu Jitsu Academy
www.ricardoalmeida.com

America's Finest Karate and Kickboxing Academy
www.afkka.org

Cranford Judo and Karate Center
www.cranfordjkc.com

Jersey Fight Club
www.jerseyfightclub.com

Kearny Martial Arts
www.kearnymartialarts.com

North Plainfield Fight Club
www.wetrainhard.com

Zealous Nation MMA
www.zealousnationmma.com

New York
Jungle Gym Martial Arts
www.junglegymbronx.com

Kioto Brazilian Jiu Jitsu
www.kiotobjjny.com

Vitor Shaolin Ribeiro Brazilian Jiu Jitsu Academy
www.vitorshaolinbjj.com

Pennsylvania
Cool Hearts Muay Thai
www.wefightsexy.com

TOUGH